BECKONED

LEARNING TO FOLLOW CHRIST

ISBN: 1539515593
ISBN 13: 9781539515593

Library of Congress Control Number: 2016917240
CreateSpace Independent Publishing Platform, North Charleston, SC

www.kristasoroka.com

 @wildforchrist

•• CONTENTS ••

My walk with Jesus Christ began in church at the age of seven and was nurtured while being raised in a Christian home in Rochester Hills, Michigan. After graduating from the University of Michigan, I spent nearly twenty years investing my time and talents in the event and hospitality management industry hosting large-scale sporting, entertainment and political events in Tampa, Florida.

While my career was blossoming, my faith was subtly declining. On June 29, 2008, I repented and recommitted my life to Jesus. The Holy Spirit beckoned me to seek God with all my heart, which meant learning how to spend extended time with Him. This began a new, wild, and undomesticated journey of faith that forever changed the course of my life.

The Holy Spirit spent the next five years preparing me, and after selling my home and giving away my possessions, on the exact day of my repentance, I was led by the Holy Spirit into the wilderness. It was during this time I learned what it meant to become a follower of Christ.

Three years and more than sixty-five thousand miles later, my spiritual walkabout taught me how to "deny myself daily" and live outside of my comfort zone. Ultimately, I found my pearl of great price, my secret to abundant living: seeking daily solitude with the heavenly Father, pursuing daily fellowship with others, and submitting daily to the will of my Creator.

I've learned to embrace God's mystery of living day by day, to trust in His love and care for me, and to practice my faith through hundreds of divine appointments. While nearing the end of my journey, the Holy Spirit laid it on my heart to share this pearl—this journey—through a weekly blog that testified to the goodness of God. For six months I shared my experiences and lessons while working out my faith, trusting that others would be inspired and encouraged as they worked out their faith too.

After pressing pause, I was led on another summer adventure across the country and moved from Coeur d'Alene, Idaho, to Brookings, South Dakota. Within days of arriving, I received direction to repurpose this collection of blogs into an inspiring guidebook of faith. While the Holy Spirit has perfectly guided my way, my prayer is that my "two fish and five loaves" will inspire you to know Jesus and guide you into a deeper walk of faith too.

What you're about to read is a three-in-one book designed to inspire you to become a follower of Christ. While every journey should begin by reading the Bible, my prayer is that this handbook will complement what He is speaking to you through His word. It begins with a collection of entries from my blog *Where He Leads* that share my real-life experiences and lessons learned while working out my faith. The book then suggests the first steps to begin your own journey. And it ends with a journal to worship God by offering your "thankful thoughts" and to record words spoken directly to you by the Holy Spirit. Consider it your personal *guidebook to faith!*

I truly believe that when you learn to become a follower of Christ by seeking and spending extended time with Him, your life will change. And when He begins to make a difference in your life, you too can make a difference in others' lives.

Will you join me by honoring Him with our lives? I'm standing with you, brothers and sisters. Heed the call of your life, get out of the boat, and begin to know Him today!

LITTLE TALBOT ISLAND STATE PARK

GAINESVILLE, FLA.

•• SECOND ACT ••

When Ben Affleck won best director for *Argo* at the 65th BAFTAs (British Academy of Film and Television Arts) awards presentation, he gave a memorable acceptance speech that alluded to his roller-coaster ride in the business. "This is a second act for me, and you have given me that…" he said. "I'm so grateful and proud, and I dedicate this to anyone else out there trying to get their second act."

Three months later I had the opportunity to host Affleck and his executive producer in Tampa on a site visit for his upcoming film *Live by Night*. After spending the day showcasing the area, we said our good-byes, and he wished me the best of luck on my upcoming journey.

I replied, "Thanks, I'm headed out to find my second act." He smiled at me and knew exactly what I was referring to.

I had shared with him that months earlier I stepped deeper into my faith journey and was led to quit working full-time after a near-twenty-year career in sports, entertainment, and politics. My director (the Holy Spirit) couldn't have given me a better script: as I sat with Hollywood's elite on the morning of Ben's site visit, I received a sales offer on my home. That was key to releasing me into the wilderness of faith.

Now, after traveling more than sixty-five thousand miles across this beautiful country on a self-funded mission trip, I find myself tucked away in Brookings, South Dakota. How did I know where to go, what to do, and to whom to minister? By relying on the Holy Spirit to lead me.

Being led required an intimate relationship with God, which meant learning how to spend extended time with Him. He promises us in Jeremiah 29:13–14: "You will seek me and find me when you seek me with all your heart. I will be found by you, declares the LORD."

By responding to His invitation, I was able to do immeasurably more than I had ever thought. He filled my life with incredible adventure and hundreds of divine appointments; he healed deep soul wounds and taught me that a true relationship is about letting go of "doing" anything for Him and simply learning to just "be" with Him. Above all, He made sure I knew He loves me.

It was like finding the pearl of great price. I had sold my home in Tampa and gave everything away to find Him! This new freedom, this intimacy, this wild adventure is the life of faith I had been longing for. He empowered me to overcome my fears, endure fiery trials, embrace His deafening silence, and allow doubt and loneliness to thoroughly run their course. And through it all, I've learned to deny Satan's lies and embrace that God is indeed a good God. He is *only* good, and His goodness triumphs over everything!

True to His goodness, after three years of devoting all my days to Him, the Holy Spirit gave me a gift and showed me my next step: "It's time to begin sharing all the lessons gathered inside your heart."

In 2015 I responded by creating a blog—my second act—to inspire wayward souls to begin seeking God with all their heart. What you're reading now is a collection of these blogs that I hope will inspire you too.

Every journey begins with a first step. I hope reading this book will be your first step toward a deeper relationship with your Creator. Will you make room for the Holy Spirit to lead you too?

And in the way Ben Affleck dedicated his directing award to those seeking a second act, I dedicate this book to those of you looking for your second act.

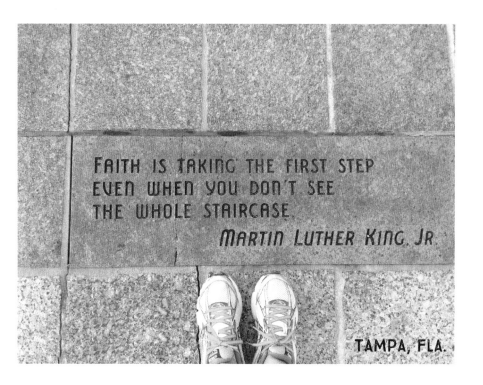

FAITH IS TAKING THE FIRST STEP EVEN WHEN YOU DON'T SEE THE WHOLE STAIRCASE.

MARTIN LUTHER KING, JR.

TAMPA, FLA.

•• THE VALUE IN PREPARING ••

December 6, 2015

I heard a wise man was once asked, "If you had five years to accomplish something, how would you spend your time?"

He responded, "I would spend four years preparing and one year doing."

On June 29, 2008, I repented and recommitted my life to Jesus Christ. It was a deeply emotional experience that changed the trajectory of my life. Immediately, the Holy Spirit began preparing me by challenging me. My first step of faith was starting a Bible study for my friends.

In His wisdom He used my friends who knew my past, saw my present, and were watching my future. He was using accountability as a key ingredient to growth and preparation.

For nearly four years, every other Tuesday night the Holy Spirit would draw His select few into my home to meet Jesus, grow in faith, and enjoy an evening of fellowship. There were lots of good times at the Fair Oaks Bible Study!

The Holy Spirit was also teaching me how to lead. He inspired me to search the New Testament scriptures to see how Jesus interacted with people. I noticed that He asked a lot of questions, so I determined I would, too.

Leading Bible study also gave me an opportunity to deepen friendships, invest in certain people for a season, and disciple others. I learned quickly that in order to disciple others I had to become a disciple first. Interestingly, this new accountability became a catalyst that trigged a desperation to seek God with all my heart.

Seeking meant practicing self-discipline. I would devote a Friday night to worshipping God, or I would challenge myself to spend an entire Saturday with Him. Some weekdays the Holy Spirit would tap me on the shoulder at 2:00 a.m., wanting fellowship. I would spend those sweet early mornings either preparing for Bible study or on my knees surrendering at the feet of Jesus.

This intentional seeking was increasing my capacity to host Him and shore up confidence that I was hearing directly from the Father. There was *value in preparing*, because in the years that lay ahead, when He would ask me to live day-to-day by His still, small voice, the journey would only be possible because He prepared me.

The enemy (who is Satan, see Matt. 13:39) wasn't happy about this new commitment, and for three years I endured unusually difficult trials in my career. But while my work life was filled with new levels of unbearable stress, my faith was catapulting. The trials that brought me to my knees were teaching me intimacy with God.

Twentieth-century evangelist Oswald Chambers writes, "A saint's life is in the hands of God like a bow and arrow in the hands of an archer. God is aiming at something the saint cannot see, and He stretches and strains, and every now and again the saint says—'I cannot stand anymore.' God does not heed, He goes on stretching till His purpose is in sight, then He lets fly. Trust yourself in God's hands."*

Will you allow the Holy Spirit to prepare you? Learn to spend extended time with Him. Only He knows where He is aiming. Trust yourself in His hands and take your first step of faith today!

*Chambers, Oswald, *My Utmost For His Highest*, Uhrichsville, Ohio (1963) p. 129

You must make a *choice* to take a *chance* or your life will never *change*.

GLACIER NATIONAL PARK

•• THREE C'S OF LIFE ••

> December 13, 2015

While living in Idaho, a friend of mine shared an inspirational quote that I felt captured the essence of my journey. It's called the Three C's of Life: choices, chances, changes. *"You must make a choice to take a chance or your life will never change."*

When I first gave my heart to Jesus at seven years old, I began my journey of faith. I loved going to church, and as I grew I began serving in multiple ministries. I also knew I loved God, attempted to connect with Him in daily devotions, and believed in prayer. But something began to stir in my spirit. There had to be more than just attending church and serving, I thought. I wanted to live the supernatural life Jesus modeled.

7

Meanwhile, I was growing frustrated with my natural life, and that frustration led to a subtle decline in my faith. By God's grace, the Holy Spirit intervened and inspired me to make a choice. I *chose* to repent and took a *chance* to pursue a deeper relationship with Jesus, and the trajectory of my life was *changed*.

The Holy Spirit invested many years preparing me and changing me to reflect the character and nature of Jesus Christ. Then He began a work to bring sweeping change in my life. How? We began working *together*:

JUNE 29, 2008: I repented and recommitted my life to Jesus. The Holy Spirit began preparing me by leading Bible study and learning how to spend extended time with Him.

FEBRUARY 2012: He inspired me to redirect my finances in preparation for the mysterious journey ahead; it required I fulfill my commitment associated with hosting the Republican National Convention, then—for the first time in my life—He asked that I stop working full-time.

NOVEMBER 1, 2012: First day without a job. He asked that I commit my "first fruits" to Him, so each morning I would begin my day by spending extended time with Him.

DECEMBER 2012: He inspired me to take a step of faith and travel up the East Coast on my first adventure. Logically, this wasn't a good decision. But walking by faith means responding to the Holy Spirit's leading and taking risks. True to His goodness, by the time I reached New York City, I had received an unexpected event management contract to work the 2013 National Collegiate Athletic Association (NCAA) Football Championship. The amount I earned was equal to the total cost of my trip. (In hindsight, this was a "trial run" to learn how He would lead me in the years ahead).

JANUARY 2013: He inspired me to clean out a guest-room closet, and then another. For the next four months, I intentionally gave away my possessions by listening for the needs around me.

APRIL 2013: He inspired me to put my house on the market. It would require a large investment (including a new roof), but He provided another unexpected contract with the Tampa Bay Film Commission that covered the cost.

MAY 2013: My heavenly Father brought me a home buyer; the selling price doubled the original purchase price eleven years earlier to provide the finances for my journey ahead.

JUNE 29, 2013: Five years to the day I recommitted my life to Jesus, I left Tampa to walk deeper into the life of faith.

JUNE 29, 2016: I heard from the Holy Spirit that my three-year mission trip was over: "Enjoy your summer! I'll provide direction for your next steps."

While those are just the highlights, do you see the underlying theme? Listening and responding to the Holy Spirit and working *together*. He's the one who presents us with choices (free will) and then inspires us to take chances that ultimately change our lives.

What choice can you make today to draw closer to Jesus? Take a chance on Him, and watch how He can change you and your life!

"LIVING CHANGE"

ROLLIN' DOWN,
NO PLACE TO GO,
LIVING TO LOVE,
LIVING TO GIVE.
LIFE PASSES BY
LIKE SAND THROUGH THE
CLOCK,
AM I WASTING TIME,
OR THE MYSTERY, DO I GET?

CHANGE I MAY,
CHANGE I MUST,
TO LIVE THIS LIFE,
TO LOVE THIS MUCH!
SURVIVE, ADAPT,
FIND THE WILL TO WIN—
AT LAST YOU OVERCOME.
AT LAST YOU LIVE!

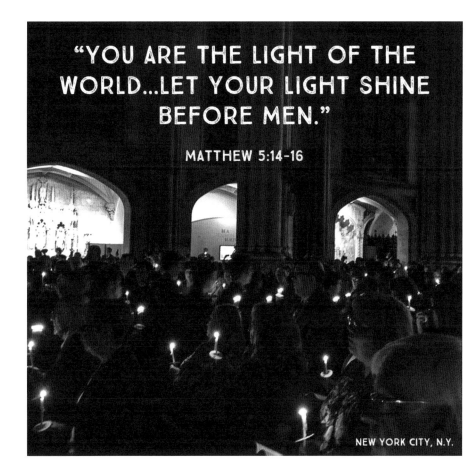

"YOU ARE THE LIGHT OF THE WORLD...LET YOUR LIGHT SHINE BEFORE MEN."

MATTHEW 5:14-16

NEW YORK CITY, N.Y.

• • SILENT NIGHT LIGHT • •

December 20, 2015

At the peak of my 2013 East Coast faith trip, I was gifted with four adventurous days in New York City. Numerous last-minute doors opened to attend Christmas performances at Times Square Church, Brooklyn Tabernacle, and even Radio City Music Hall to see the Rockettes! I strolled by the festive window displays, admired Rockefeller Center's famous Christmas tree, and eventually wandered into one of my favorite destinations: St. Patrick's Cathedral.

The reverent atmosphere quieted my soul and beckoned me to settle in a seat behind numerous roped-off pews. To my surprise Mass began, but the event planner in me was distracted, wondering, why the limited seating? When I got up to leave, I asked the New York Police Department officer stationed at the entrance for an explanation.

"The annual Christmas performance is tonight," he answered. "If you want to attend, come back in an hour and find me."

"Sure!" I said, impressed with God's streak of perfect timing!

When I returned I was surprised I could find him in the now standing-room-only crowd.

"Are you ready? Follow me," he said, while removing the center-aisle security rope, escorting me past numerous onlookers. I felt like a VIP as we drew closer to the front, where he finally sat me, my head spinning—so grateful, so blessed, so amazed I was there!

The service was lovely, the performances heavenly, and the experience epic. At one point in the service a single flame was lit. That one flame lit each attendee's candles until the lights-out cathedral was gloriously illuminated with single flames. We joined our voices in singing "Silent Night," and I was grateful for the gift of heavenly peace—even if for a moment—before our flames were eventually extinguished.

I was recently reminded of that special night while reading about a fourth-century man named Paulinus, who, realizing that his civilization was crashing to destruction, decided that "the only thing he could do was to keep alight a lamp in a particular shrine, and that's what he decided to do."*

It was Paulinus's "Silent Night" light; his way of saying that the opposite is true.

Our civilization is crashing to destruction, too. We light our single flames, perform random acts of kindness, and check off our "feel-good" box. But then what? We finish singing "Silent Night," and our flames go out, extinguishing the only light the dark world around us may see.

What if we allow the Holy Spirit not only to light our flame but lead us to *keep* it burning? *Keep* it burning by daily reading God's Word, seeking fellowship with believers, and giving thanks for the goodness of God. The world desperately needs you to keep alight your flame. Consider it your "Silent Night" light; your way of saying the opposite is true.

*Muggeridge, Malcolm, Speech at Church of Saint Mary the Great, Cambridge, UK, May 7, 1967.

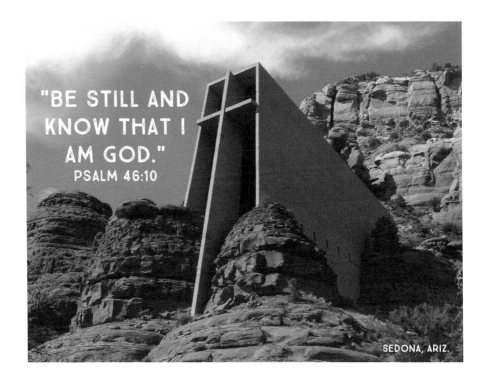

"BE STILL AND KNOW THAT I AM GOD."
PSALM 46:10

SEDONA, ARIZ.

•• THE NEW DEFAULT ••

December 27, 2015

The Holy Spirit led me into a new way of living, or, as I call it, my new default.

I default to being with God.

Early in my faith walk, I made an attempt to be with Him: an hour-long service on Sunday, a quick ten-minute daily devotional, maybe even a "bless me and others" prayer on the way to work.

After I recommitted my life, I decided to honor Him by reprioritizing my time and thoughts. Enter coffee! I offered the first moments of my day by practicing daily devotions at Starbucks. It was there the Holy Spirit poured into me, and out of His overflow, I began pouring into others! Divine appointments—meetings set up by the Holy Spirit to speak life into others—became abundant.

While offering my mornings was essential to both enter and endure the sometime harsh environment of the wilderness—living without friends and family and relying completely on God—I noticed I was struggling during the evenings. Loneliness and doubt were constant companions. I tried distracting myself with outdoor adventure and entertainment, but the Holy Spirit quietly intervened: "You've been faithful in having great mornings; I need you to have better nights."

Exit television. Enter more time with God.

Initially it was difficult. I was already starved for social fellowship and eliminating distraction would expose my loneliness even further. I was struggling against despair as I entered my third year on this journey without some type of visible breakthrough in my circumstances. My friend Lynn endured a desperate call on Christmas that year when I called her, lamenting that God hadn't shown up, wondering has He forgotten me, how can He ask me to keep doing this, and now He wants me to spend more time with Him?

I'm dying!

Exactly.

Galatians 2:20 says, "I have been crucified with Christ. It is no longer I who lives, but Christ lives in me. The life I now live in the body I live by faith in the Son of God who loved me and gave Himself for me."

God was asking me to die to self. In His wisdom He led me to the Northwest—as far away from Florida as one can get and still be in the contiguous United States—where I had no identity. No one knew me, my talents, my likes, or my background. I was enduring the death to self—a life without an identity—so I could find my identity in Christ. It was like finding the sweet spot of faith.

It's been years since practicing my new default and the benefit is simple: I'm always with God. It's taken great discipline to keep turning my thoughts toward Him. I've gained strength in both mind and will, but the benefit has been continuous peace, comfort, and strength for this wild journey of faith.

I think back often to a service I attended in 2013 at the Chapel of the Holy Cross in Sedona, Arizona. The order of service included the following song: "Be Still and Know That I Am God. Be Still and Know. Be Still. Be."

Will you allow the Holy Spirit to lead you to a new default? Consider removing the distractions in your life today and take a step toward just being with God.

And if it helps, drink more coffee!

"HOLD ON"

WHEN LIFE LETS YOU DOWN,
WHEN TEARS BLIND YOUR WAY,
WHEN DARKNESS ABOUNDS,
THERE'S NO WORDS LEFT TO SAY.

WHEN YOUR WAY IS UNCLEAR,
YOUR PATH NOT YET SEEN,
WHEN YOU CAN'T SEE AHEAD,
IT'S SO HARD TO BELIEVE.

JUST HOLD ON; DON'T LET GO.
HOLD ON, WATCH, AND PRAY.
THERE'S STRENGTH LEFT INSIDE;
THERE'S HOPE ON THE WAY.

HIS WORD IS THE LIGHT.
HIS TRUTH IS THE WAY.
HIS LOVE HOLDS YOU TIGHT.
HIS PROMISES PRAY.

WHEN YOU'RE WEAK AND UNSURE
AND YOUR HEART LOST ITS WAY,
LOOK UP SEE HIS LIGHT,
WATCH YOUR DARK BECOME DAY.

DIG DEEP DOWN INSIDE.
WORK THROUGH THE PAIN.
HE'S THERE BY YOUR SIDE.
HE'S LIFTING YOUR WEIGHT.

JUST HOLD ON; DON'T LET GO.
HOLD ON, WATCH, AND PRAY.
THERE'S STRENGTH LEFT INSIDE.
THERE'S HOPE ON THE WAY.

HIS WORD IS THE LIGHT.
HIS TRUTH IS THE WAY.
HIS LOVE HOLDS YOU TIGHT.
HIS PROMISES PRAY.

JUST HOLD ON; DON'T LET GO.
HOLD ON, WATCH, AND PRAY
THERE'S STRENGTH LEFT INSIDE.
THERE'S HOPE ON THE WAY.

> *"Be holy, because I, the Lord your God, am holy."*
> *Leviticus 14:1*

THEODORE ROOSEVELT NATIONAL PARK

•• THE PURSUIT OF HOLINESS ••

> *January 3, 2016*

I was driving along Theodore Roosevelt National Park's thirty-six-mile scenic Loop Drive when I first encountered wild horses descending on rolling hills. To my surprise, one gently positioned itself parallel to my vehicle. In response, I opened my windows and paced my car and my heart with this magnificent animal, wild and undomesticated.

Something changed in me that day. I was only weeks into my wild and undomesticated walk of faith, blind to my purpose, and learning to live day by day. It wasn't until years later, when reading a definition of holiness, that the Holy Spirit would reveal what lit my fire that day: "Holiness isn't a bland attribute of God. It's wild and undomesticated. Holiness is an interior fire, a passion for living for God, a capacity for exuberance in living out the life of God in the details of our day-to-day lives. Holy is not a word that drains the blood out of life. It's a word that gets our blood pumping."*

That was it! I was in full pursuit of holiness!

Not happiness.

I've been told repeatedly by people that I seem happy, but the truth is my journey has not led me to a life of happiness. Learning to follow Jesus isn't exactly a walk in the park! It takes strength and resolve to endure times of loneliness, rejection, and disappointment.

But following Christ is the greatest choice I have ever made. It's passionate, wild, mysterious, consuming, and, well, holy! I'm alive so His purposes can be fulfilled in me!

Do you have that same fire in you, that same capacity to live for Jesus? Or are you on the sidelines, doubtful, tentative? What is keeping you from getting in the game?

Giving over and living your life for Christ doesn't mean just doing things for Him. Over-committing can often drain you. It means releasing control to your Creator so He can fulfill His purpose in you. Pursuing the holy life God has called you to means your blood pumps and your fire is lit to live for Him every day!

I hope you join me in pursuing holiness. I encourage you to read the definition again, and let it define the kind of Father you want to serve. The kind of Jesus you want to follow. And the kind of Holy Spirit you want leading you.

*Peterson, Eugene, *The Message Ministry Edition: The Bible in Contemporary Language*, Colorado Springs, Co (2002) p. 177

"Yet, O LORD, you are our Father. We are the clay, you are the potter; we are all the work of your hand."
Isaiah 64:8

WHISTLER, B.C., CANADA

•• TRUE PURPOSE ••

> January 10, 2016

While reading John Eldredge's book *Wild at Heart*, I was challenged to put aside my false self and find my true name in Christ.

I took time to reflect while on a ski trip in Whistler, British Columbia, when the Holy Spirit led me back to my childhood. You wouldn't know it from how I am today, but I was a very fearful child, afraid of people, of animals, and adventure. I stuck to my mom like glue. Most saw me as shy, but deep down I was always afraid. In my adult life, fear turned into anxiety. For years I dealt with anxiety attacks, a physical anxiousness that Satan used to keep me locked up inside my false self.

But God.

The Bible tells us that He is the potter, and we are the clay (Isa. 64:8). My heavenly Father—the potter who created me before time began—knew His purpose for me: to affect people's lives for eternity. Through His love and grace, He inspired me to repent and seek Him with all my heart. By pursuing Him I was empowered to overcome anxiety and fear so I could live wild at heart on this new journey of faith!

Would you also consider laying aside your false self and pursuing Jesus? Only He can release you from fears, empower you to lay aside your false self, and give you grace to live your true purpose.

And don't worry—you're not alone. Even Superman needed a reminder.

There is a scene in the 2013 film *Man of Steel* in which Clark Kent's dad reveals that Clark is not from this world.

The young Clark struggles with this revelation and would rather pretend it's not true. His dad wisely reminds him that he has another Father who gave him another name and sent him to earth for a reason. And even if it took Clark the rest of his life, he owed it to himself to find out what that reason is.

When you're born again, you enter into a relationship with another father— the heavenly Father. He gave you another name. And He sent you here for a reason. And even if it takes you the rest of your life, you owe it to yourself to find out what that reason is.

I found mine. My name is Krista, follower of Christ.

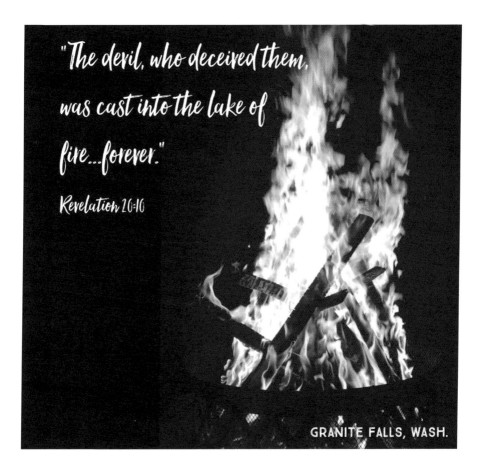

"The devil, who deceived them, was cast into the lake of fire...forever."

Revelation 20:16

GRANITE FALLS, WASH.

•• RING OF FIRE ••

January 17, 2016

I kicked off 2016 by stepping into the ring with the enemy, and it got ugly.

It began on January 2 at a gas station, when the Holy Spirit led me to anonymously give money to a family whose vehicle's windows had been smashed out. I pulled away praying that God's mighty name be glorified and for the family's faith to be renewed. Then I didn't think twice about it.

A week later, while living wild at heart on my trip to British Columbia, the enemy retaliated. He saw that my visit was more than a fun adventure; it was a mission trip, full of divine appointments to both testify about the goodness of God and to test my character.

He hated it, so he hit back, and I became the victim of a smash-and-grab in downtown Vancouver, where someone shattered my rear passenger window and stole my suitcase. It was like Satan was saying, "Window for window. You hit me; I'll hit you back." There is some serious bad blood between us!

On my drive home to northern Idaho, I was reminded of a scene in the 2006 film *Rocky Balboa* in which Rocky coaches his son on the realities of life outside the ring. He reminds him that taking hits in the ring is like taking hits in life. If you're tough enough to endure and keep moving forward, then you set yourself up for a win! But victory is only for those willing to take the hits.

Are you taking hits in your life? Are you tired of losing, getting beat to your knees? Do you want to win this week? It all starts by knowing your enemy and his strategies.

Satan uses different tactics to hit you and keep you from moving forward in faith. Maybe you're hesitant to believe in Jesus? That's doubt. Do you find it difficult to spend time alone with Him? That's distraction. Do you blame God for your feelings of abandonment? That's deceit. Are you rejecting Him because of a past wound in a church? That's division. Are you frustrated that you can't kick a bad habit? That's discouragement. Feeling confused? Shamed? Insecure? Hit! Hit! Hit!

The good news is Jesus has all the authority and power to help you overcome, because He has defeated Satan! The Bible teaches us the enemy's destiny is already determined: "The devil, who deceived them, was cast into the lake of fire and brimstone…forever" (Rev. 20:10).

By entering into a personal relationship with Jesus, you can overcome, too. There is power in the name of Jesus to get back up and move forward. Will you seek Him this week by spending extended time getting to know Him? Only He can change your life.

And know that I'm in your corner cheering you on!

"NOW FAITH IS BEING SURE OF WHAT WE HOPE FOR AND CERTAIN OF WHAT WE DO NOT SEE."

HEBREWS 11:1

COEUR D'ALENE, IDAHO

•• ENCOURAGING YOURSELF ••

January 24, 2016

A friend of mine asked if he could come over for project night one evening, which really meant, "Do you mind if I turn your apartment into my wood shop?" Ha! I was more than happy to.

I asked what he was making, and while he was full of ideas, one of his ideas in particular inspired me. Hanging on my wall, I had two wooden signs with the words "Faith" and "Love," so I decided to finish the trifecta by creating one that said "Hope" (1 Cor. 13:13).

I took advantage of God's "free Home Depot" on a hike that week and searched for the right piece of wood. I hiked up and down diligently searching, veering on and off the path, with no luck.

On my third and final lap down, I prayed, "Holy Spirit, lead me to hope." It was almost prophetic.

He answered halfway down, where I turned to the right and saw a small ditch covered with branches. Buried underneath was the piece of wood that would become my hope board. I stopped to give thanks for a big answer to a small prayer.

I took time to consider that for much of the year, my hope was buried in a ditch, and I often wondered if I could endure another lap up this mountain called my life. But while Satan was using his strategy of despair to keep me buried, the Holy Spirit was working all things together for my good and taught me a key spiritual discipline of faith.

He reminded me of David's journey in the wilderness, and I began to draw inspiration from this man after God's own heart. Misunderstood? Lonely? Living in fear? The same guy who made lamenting famous in the Psalms was simultaneously teaching us to always keep our hope in God.

But how?

It was in the wilderness that David learned to encourage himself.

The Bible says, "Now faith is being sure of what we hope for, certain of what we do not see" (Heb. 11:1). Too often we rely on the tangible structure of religion—a Sunday-morning service, a Tuesday-night Bible study, a fill-in-the-blank church sign-up sheet—and we call it our faith.

But what happens when you remove the religious structure from your life? Are you *sure* of the Jesus you claim to hope in? Are you *certain* of the God you don't see?

When you learn to encourage yourself in the faith, like David, you begin to light your own fires. You intentionally seek God every day in all things because you passionately believe in Him and trust that all of His promises are true, no matter what your circumstances look like.

Oswald Chambers writes, "Faith is not a pathetic sentiment but robust vigorous confidence built on the fact that God is holy love. You cannot see Him just now, you cannot understand what He is doing, but you know Him…Faith is the heroic effort of your life, you fling yourself in reckless confidence on God."*

Will you take your first step today and resolve to encourage yourself in the faith?

*Chambers, Oswald, *My Utmost For His Highest*, Uhrichsville, Ohio (1963) p. 129

"REPENT AND BE BAPTIZED, EVERY ONE OF YOU, IN THE NAME OF JESUS CHRIST FOR THE FORGIVENESS OF YOUR SINS. AND YOU WILL RECEIVE THE GIFT OF THE HOLY SPIRIT."

ACTS 2:38

ZION NATIONAL PARK

•• INSIDE PRESENCE ••

January, 31, 2016

I love sports. I spent most of my career in sports management and enjoyed feeding off the camaraderie of teamwork, the athletes' self-disciplined grind to push beyond physical limits, the electric atmosphere of arenas and stadiums, and the dedication of families and fans! I especially love University of Michigan sports and often keep tabs on my alma matter's teams to fuel my fandom.

I was inspired when reading about power forward, Mark Donnal, one of the least-recognized players on Michigan's basketball team, who exploded onto the Big Ten Conference during the 2015-2016 season. When his teammates were asked about his growing impact on the team, they echoed the same sentiment: "Inside presence."

They saw that when he believed in himself and played confidently, it took their team to the next level.

I immediately thought of the Holy Spirit as our "inside presence."

He's our power forward and our O-line, our goalie and our tag-team partner. He's what Mickey and Duke were to Rocky Balboa, what Billy Beane was to the Oakland Athletics. He stays in our enemy's face to block his shots and trains and challenges us to take ourselves and our team to the next level.

You may not be on a sports team, but if you've accepted Jesus as your Savior, you're on God's team, and His team is His family. We all have roles to play and we need each other to take our team (family) to the next level. Satan is our opponent and comes at us with a fiery offensive plan to defeat us, but the Holy Spirit—our inside presence—is always there to help us.

This doesn't happen magically. We cheat ourselves and our family if we don't participate on the team.

I experienced the importance of teamwork earlier that week. Just hours after publishing the previous week's blog "Encouraging Yourself," the enemy hit me with a wave of doubt: "Do you really believe God cares for you? What is your faith founded on? Can you prove it?" Seriously, I wanted to pummel him!

But I couldn't do it on my own. I texted a teammate/friend of mine, "Hey, can you throw some punches in your prayers tonight?"

He responded, "I just put on my gloves, tapping you out now!"

His prayers supernaturally freed me to hear directly from Jesus that night and into the next day. My friend defended me, so I could receive God's direction without having to beat back the enemy myself. (This was an answer to a prayer. Just weeks earlier, I asked by faith for someone to "lay down cover against the enemy so I can fulfill my mission!").

We are all wired to accomplish God's mission and it's up to us to figure out what that is. While I write this, I'm the one laying down cover for another friend who has fallen back into an old habit and needs to tap into the power of the Holy Spirit.

If you're wondering how you can receive the Holy Spirit, open your ears to hear what Peter teaches in Acts 2:38: "Repent and be baptized, every one of you, in the name of Jesus Christ for the forgiveness of your sins. And you will receive the gift of the Holy Spirit."

If you haven't accepted Jesus, on behalf of the family of God we invite you into our family! If you're already family, I encourage you to "lay down cover" for a friend, or put on your gloves and "tap out" a brother or sister this week. We all need each other!

BOZEMAN, MONT.

"HOME"

GOT THE MOON AT MY BACK,
SUN IN MY EYES–
ROADS STRETCHED FOR MILES
AND MOUNTAINS PILED HIGH.

BUT ONE THING'S FOR CERTAIN–
TWO THINGS I KNOW–
WHEN I CAN'T FIND MY WAY,
I CAN ALWAYS FIND CHRIST.

I CAMP IN THE WOODS
AND WALK ON THE BEACH,
RUN ON THE TRAILS,
MY HEART OUT OF REACH.

IN CHRIST IS MY FAMILY.
HIS FRIENDS ARE MINE TOO.
HOME IS WITH CHRIST,
AND CHRIST IS IN YOU.

I'M SEARCHING FOR HOME,
A PLACE STRETCHED OUT WIDE.
I'M SEARCHING FOR LOVE,
SEARCHING FOR LIFE.

NO MATTER YOUR TRAVELS,
YOUR ROADS, OR YOUR LIVES,
CHRIST CALLS YOU HOME,
AND HOME IS ALIVE.

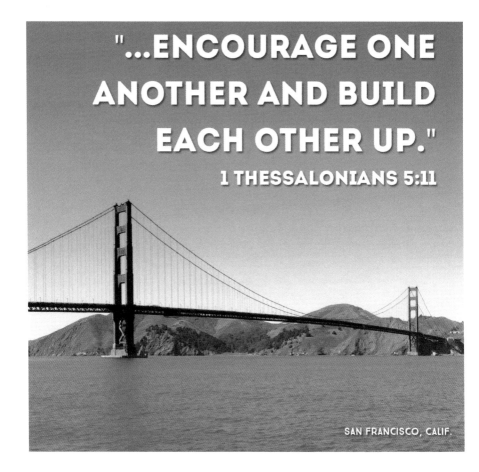

> ## "...ENCOURAGE ONE ANOTHER AND BUILD EACH OTHER UP."
> ### 1 THESSALONIANS 5:11

SAN FRANCISCO, CALIF.

•• GAME OF INCHES ••

February 7, 2016

While working hospitality events at Super Bowl 50, I decided a good old-fashioned do-or-die coach's speech would encourage people's faith, and who better to motivate us than the gritty and passionate Al Pacino?

In the film *Any Given Sunday*, Pacino's character, Coach Tony D'Amato, is desperate to motivate his football players, who are performing only for themselves. He knows they're broken and have little chance to win unless he can provide them with the right game plan. His solution is a speech for them to either heal as a team or die as individuals. It's up to each of them to decide.

He reminds his players that life is a *game of inches* and charges them—as a team—to fight for that inch because when adding up those inches it will make the difference between a win or a loss.

Our teammates are made up of the family of God, and we're broken and in need of healing. Individualism, selfishness, and pride have infected our family. We can choose to heal as a family—by remembering we're on the same turf fighting the same enemy—or die as individuals. The good news is Jesus already won the championship for us! But before He returns for His trophy (us), He asks us to live as a family.

I encourage you to look at your teammates around you. Are you seeing people who will sacrifice for you? Would you do the same for them? If you're like me, I've incurred injuries from selfish teammates in the past. By God's grace, He healed my wounds, inspired me to pursue healthy relationships, and kept me in the game to fight for His family!

Will you join me in healing as a family this week? Inch by inch, person by person, will you sacrifice for your teammates by taking time to pray for someone? Sending someone a note of encouragement? Hosting a friend for coffee and Bible study? Picking up the tab for someone in need? It's up to you to reach out.

Now, what are you gonna do?

TRUST
IN THE LORD
WITH ALL YOUR HEART
PROVERBS 3:5

BIG MOUNTAIN, WHITEFISH, MONT.

•• PERFECTLY LOVED ••

>February 14, 2016<

It finally happened. When I least expected it, my heavenly Father, who has been relentlessly pursuing me, showed me He loves me. Perfectly.

His pursuit began the day of my "white funeral" (as Oswald Chambers writes), when the Holy Spirit led me to truly repent. He continued through early morning devotions during my five years of preparation; then He beckoned me across His wild and beautiful country for four months and ultimately led me into years of solitude, teaching me to know Him by waiting on Him. All along He was showing me He loved me. Perfectly.

Oh, it didn't always feel like love. But the problem wasn't on His end; it was on mine. He was my carpenter, methodically stripping me down to the studs and exposing a serious crack in my foundation and making me ask, "Do I *know* He loves me?". I didn't, so He gently informed me, "We're not going any further until we fix this."

You see, my idea of being loved was very different than His. I carry a deep sorrow in my heart, and many times I've doubted God's goodness. But all along He was working to expose an idol in my life by testing me: Would I continue serving Him when (it felt like) He was withholding His goodness from me? Do I love *Him*? Or do I love Him only to receive His blessings and gifts? Loaded questions.

His renovation started on a Friday morning in late October when a wave of sadness overwhelmed my heart. The Holy Spirit invited me to seek the Father, so I spent an entire day on my sofa, pursuing Him through worshipping, reading, journaling, sitting, listening, and waiting on Him… until 4:00 a.m.! I spent Saturday with friends, believing He was working on my behalf even though my heart was still tender. By Sunday afternoon, during moments of reflection and giving thanks for all He's done in my life, my eyes were finally opened:

He's trustworthy. And when I trust Him, I know He loves me.

When I looked back and saw His faithfulness and protection and provision, His gentle leading along unknown adventurous paths, His opened and closed doors, and His beauty and His wildness, He was showing me that He is worthy of my trust. Proverbs 3:5 reminds us to "trust in the Lord with all your heart…" Why? Because He is our Father and He is always working for the good of His children.

Armed with this new truth, I was tested immediately. Familiar disappointments flared up, but I began denying my circumstances and *trusted* that He was working them for my good. The result? Peace! Not long afterward, I felt excluded and then used, but I fought back and told God I *trusted* that He was using it for His glory. The result? Peace! Then I was tempted to look into my future—with an expiring lease on my apartment and an unknown path ahead—but I stood firm, *trusting* He would go before me and be with me every step of the way. The result? Peace! This one truth supernaturally laid a new foundation and empowered me to overcome the enemy—a foundation built on the assurance that He's always good.

Do you trust God? Do you know that He loves you? Or do you find yourself asking: How could God let this happen? Why doesn't He do something? If God loves me, why am I going through this? Doesn't He care? Don't be fooled, it's the enemy we should question: "Who are *you*"? Since Satan first spoke doubt in the Garden of Eden, our minds have been filled with it.

I challenge you today to reflect on your past and see how God has loved you. Can you see His goodness? He is the beginning and the end, and everything in between is good! Will you begin trusting Him, so you can walk in peace knowing you are loved, *perfectly?*

COLMAN, S.D.

"LEAN IN"

"BREATHE," HE SAID,
"JUST BREATHE, AND LET GO.
YOU'RE HOLDING IT ALL IN.
YOU'RE CARRYING A HEAVY
LOAD."

I DON'T KNOW HOW.
WHO CAN I TRUST?
MY HEART IS SCARRED.
MY HANDS ARE ROUGH.

THEN HE LEANED IN.
HE SHOWED ME HOW.
HE OFFERED HIS LOVE.
HE GIVES IT NOW.

LEAN IN; LET GO
WHEN YOU FEEL ALONE.
LEAN IN; LET GO.
HE'S STRONG; HE'LL HOLD.
LEAN IN! AND LET GO!
YOU'RE ALMOST HOME.
LEAN IN; LET GO.
LEAN IN. LET GO.

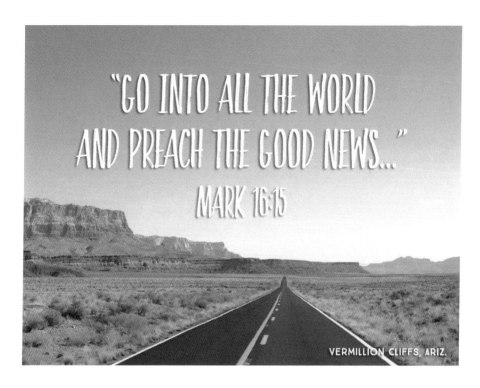

"GO INTO ALL THE WORLD AND PREACH THE GOOD NEWS..."

MARK 16:15

VERMILLION CLIFFS, ARIZ.

• •TURNING THE TABLES• •

February 21, 2016

I had an epiphany the week I wrote this blog and, inspired by the Holy Spirit, I created a *Where He Leads* Facebook page to coincide with my blog.

It happened when reading a story about Kirk Cousins, the Washington Redskins quarterback, who, when faced with impending contract negotiations, took a step of faith and gave his best effort for the 2015 season, trusting that God would be faithful to His Word (Prov. 3:5–6). He asked Him to "turn the tables," and Kirk's season was blessed beyond his wildest dreams. God turned a position of disadvantage into one of advantage.

Like Kirk, I asked God to do the same for me.

Those who know me understand my aversion to social media. I've always seen it as a distraction from concentrating on my walk with Jesus. When I read God's Word reminding us of "the cravings of sinful man, the lust of his eyes, and the boasting of what he has and does" (1 John 2:16), I automatically think Facebook, Twitter, and Instagram! These are major red flags in my faith walk.

But the Holy Spirit checked me and reminded me of the Great Commission: "Go into all the world and preach the good news" (Mark 16:15). He opened my eyes, and asked me to pray as Kirk prayed. Even though I saw social media as a disadvantage, I asked Him to *turn the tables* and make it into an advantage. I decided to trust that His anointing would rest on this platform to reach more people with the good news of Jesus Christ than I could imagine in my wildest dreams!

While this may seem trivial to most (you might be wondering, "What have you been waiting for, Krista?"), I challenge you to think of your own faith walk. Is there a trivial area of your life—a disadvantage—that by God's turning the tables can be turned into an advantage to further *His* kingdom? Maybe you want to go on a mission trip but don't have the funds, or you want to volunteer but don't have the time, or maybe you feel powerless and alone and are thinking, "What can I possibly do?"

I encourage you to pray God's Word back to Him: "You told me to go into all the world, so show me what that looks like in my life!" Remember that Jesus ultimately *turned the tables* for us through his death, resurrection, and ascension. He redeemed us and empowered us to live victoriously here on earth so we can do all things through Christ who strengthens us! (Phil. 4:13).

Will you ask the Holy Spirit to lead you into the Great Commission this week? I'm standing with you, waiting to see how God turns the tables in your life!

• • • •

Going into all the world, can be as simple as doing the next thing: making eye contact with the next person you walk by and smiling, or asking the grocery-store cashier how he or she is today. Will you serve Jesus by living an others-centered life?

• • • •

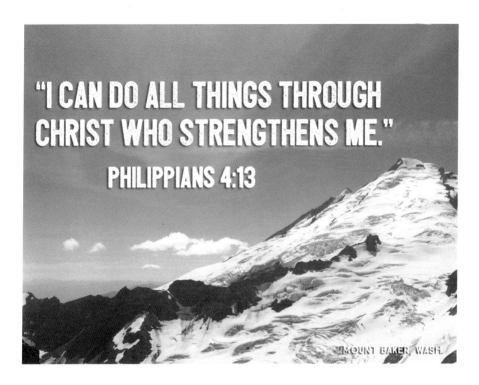

"I CAN DO ALL THINGS THROUGH CHRIST WHO STRENGTHENS ME."

PHILIPPIANS 4:13

MOUNT BAKER, WASH.

•• ALL YOUR STRENGTH ••

February 28, 2016

I watched the 1985 film *Rocky IV* one winter evening and couldn't go to sleep afterward. Strangely, I felt like going for a run up a mountain in knee-deep snow while KGB limos tracked me!

Possibly the best of the seven films in the series, Rocky's determination to avenge the death of his friend Apollo Creed is aided by one of the most underrated characters in the film series: Duke Evers.

Originally Apollo's trainer, Duke transitions to Rocky's corner in *Rocky III*, when he fights "Clubber" Lang. After Apollo dies, he travels to Siberia with Rocky for epic training sessions prior to fighting his opponent, Drago.

Once in the ring, Duke does his best to *will* Rocky to a win. He injects confidence in his exhausted fighter; motivates him to deny his pain, and reminds him that to win he has to knock Drago out by giving it *all* his strength, *all* his power and *all* his love!

I was thinking how I'd like to have Duke in my corner. Not just during a hard workout, but, you know, when I wake up in the morning. "Krista, life is going to be tough today, but you got this! People are going to disappoint you, you'll have to train on your own, and it's going to hurt. But, look, you cut the enemy this week! You hurt him! You start, and don't stop today! Give it *all* your strength, *all* your power, and *all* your love! Remember, no pain! *No* pain! *No pain!*"

Then I realized I have someone better than Duke. I have the Holy Spirit! He is always in our corner, inspiring and empowering us to overcome the enemy's hits. If you're a believer, each day you step into the ring of fire, take hits, get knocked down, or, worse, knocked out. You may be disappointed, misunderstood, lonely, discouraged, or just worn out from the fight of faith.

But so was Jesus Christ. In fact, He was worse than we could ever imagine. He took the worst hits Satan could give to the point of suffering and death on the cross. But just when it looked like He was knocked out, He turned the tables, defeated death, and rose again! The ultimate comeback!

Through His death, resurrection and ascension, we're empowered to not only fight in the same ring, but to overcome and win. The Bible says, "I can do all things through Christ who strengthens me." (Phil. 4:13). Why? So we can glorify all Jesus has done for us!

Tony Burton, who played Duke, passed away the week I wrote this blog. Just as Duke inspired Rocky to keep Apollo's spirit alive and make sure he didn't die in vain, I challenge you to hear God speaking to you about your part in keeping Jesus's victory on the cross alive. You may take some hits along the way, and it may take *all* your strength, *all* your power, and *all* your love. But don't forget, if you've given your life to Jesus, your Duke, the Holy Spirit, is in your corner!

And so am I!

MT. BAKER, WASH.

"PRESS ON"

NOT WHAT I DID,
BUT WHO I AM.
NOT WHAT WAS,
BUT WHAT IS.

RELIVING THE PAST
KEEPS A LIFE CONFINED.
LIVING NOW
BRINGS JOY AND SMILES!

LEARN FROM THE PAST.
FAILURES, BUILD ON.
BREAK THE CHAINS.
KEEP PRESSING ON.

LOOK TO THE FUTURE.
KEEP LOOKING AHEAD.
BELIEVE AND TRUST
THAT GOD KNOWS BEST.

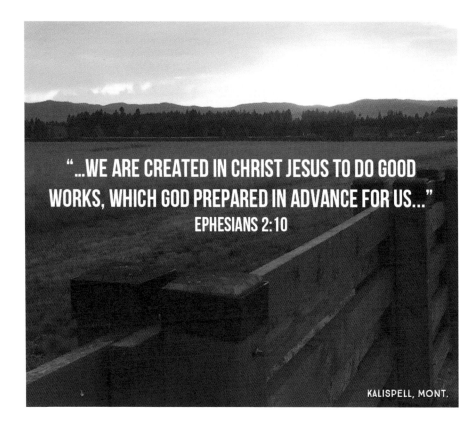

> "...WE ARE CREATED IN CHRIST JESUS TO DO GOOD WORKS, WHICH GOD PREPARED IN ADVANCE FOR US..."
>
> EPHESIANS 2:10

KALISPELL, MONT.

•• DIVINE APPOINTMENTS ••

March 6, 2016

I live for divine appointments. Holy Spirit–coordinated encounters, Heaven-meets-earth kind of moments.

They're anointed "snapshots" in life when you say, "Wow, did that just happen?" and are reminded that not only is God in control of everything, but He loves using us to reach others!

I first noticed them years ago when settling into my Tampa neighborhood Starbucks for devotions. Fellow coffee lovers seemed *drawn* to my study area, and before I knew it the Holy Spirit opened doors to speak God's truth into their lives. At first it seemed bizarre! But as I continued to pursue Jesus—by reading my Bible and spending extended time getting to know Him—I learned to discern His voice and respond to these opportunities by faith. Hundreds of divine appointments later—in coffee shops and department stores, on airplanes and hikes—I can testify to the exhilarating feeling of joy these opportunities offer!

What are these appointments? They're more than random acts of kindness or doing good deeds. Each is centered around sharing the love of Jesus. The Holy Spirit may prompt you to speak an encouraging scripture to a coworker, or be called on to defend God's truths with a family member, or even pray with someone on the spot in a public place! There's usually one common thread: you have to be bold and brave to testify of your faith in God.

After having coffee with a friend this particular week, I was encouraged by his recent divine appointment. While harvesting corn in South Dakota, he noticed a vehicle stalled on the side of the road and felt a prompting from the Holy Spirit. In his words: "'You ever get those moments when God so clearly states your next move in life?"

He decided to hop off his tractor, jump the fence and ask if the man needed help. The result? He spent a half hour sharing God's love with Harry, an elderly Vietnam vet, who didn't think the Lord had anything good in store for him. My friend said, "You're wrong, He absolutely does!" and while waiting for a tow service, he took Harry's hands and prayed words of encouragement for him. How divine!

When you learn to live an "others-centered" life you open yourself up for opportunities. The Holy Spirit will coordinate them; you just need to respond by taking a step of faith. As a believer, you were designed to live this way! Ephesians 2:10 reminds us: "For we are God's workmanship, created in Christ Jesus to do good works, which God prepared in advance for us to do."

Sometimes, that good work may be pivotal to where someone spends eternity.

Just a year earlier, I was led to my most impactful divine appointment while sitting at my local Idaho Starbucks. I met Jason, a passionate and charismatic guy who had turned from his Christian faith. God saddled me up next to him for what would become a months-long, daily assignment to remind him about God's love and faithfulness. Tragically, just months later, he would pass away.*

Will you *hop off your tractor* or *saddle up* next to someone when the Holy Spirit leads you into a divine appointment this week? It may be in the lunchroom of your office, at a coffeehouse, in the grocery store, or across your neighbor's fence. There are Jasons and Harrys in our lives every day. As my friend says, "When God tugs on your heart to do something, simply do it, be bold. Every life is valuable…"

This blog was dedicated to Jason Gritten. Thanks for reaching for the boat of believers.

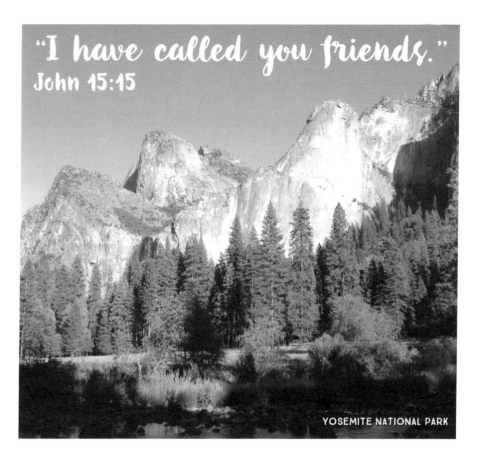

"*I have called you friends.*"
John 15:15

YOSEMITE NATIONAL PARK

•• JESUS FRIENDS ••

>March 13, 2016<

I laughed all day long one Sunday. Unplanned, I spent the entire day with new friends and at times laughed so hard I couldn't talk!

I kept wondering all day what made this group of close friends so special. They're incredibly talented, smart, fun, and have hearts of gold, but there was something more to their friendship. And then I realized they're bonded together because of their faith in Christ. They're "Jesus Friends!"

In the age of social media, it's no secret that authentic friendships are declining. The enemy is artificially manipulating relationships, telling us our identity is based on how many virtual likes we have. Liar, liar. We need to remember who *liked* us first: Jesus!

The Bible reminds us that Jesus is not only the author of friendship but includes us as friends: "I have called you friends" (John 15:15). When you know Him as your friend, you can be a friend.

But first, you need to know *Him*.

Who is He? He's loving, loyal, and a great listener. He's funny and fierce, gracious and good. He's kind and considerate, wild and wonderful! He offers perfect advice (only when asked!), and never fails or disappoints.

He's amazing!

He's a giver, not a taker; has big shoulders to lean on, and wipes away all our tears. He always protects us and never shames us. He's tough on our hearts when we need discipline, then whispers softly when we need comfort. He's our brother, our Savior, and our soon-coming King!

Do you know Him in this way? As creations of God, we *long to belong* to His family. By accepting Jesus in your heart, you can experience friendship, family and fellowship at its best…how God created it! Your new friendships with the family God puts in your life will all have Jesus as the common denominator.

This is what I experienced that Sunday. Out of our personal relationships with Jesus, came fun adventure, deep conversation, and jokes for days! We were all in fellowship as brothers and sisters in Christ.

Are you missing this kind of fellowship in your life? As believers, God intends us to live as family. This will probably look different than you think. But if you allow the Holy Spirit to lead you into Godly fellowship this week, who knows, maybe you'll laugh all day long too!

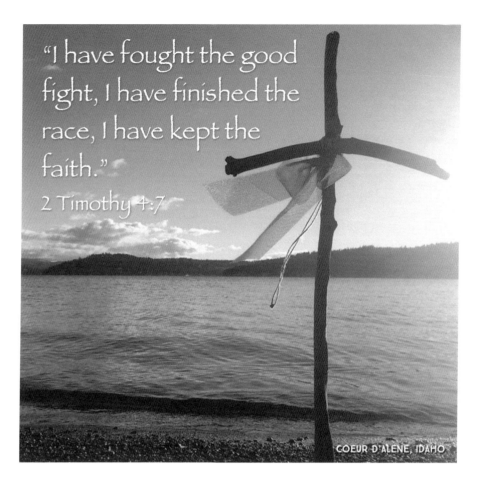

"I have fought the good fight, I have finished the race, I have kept the faith."

2 Timothy 4:7

COEUR D'ALENE, IDAHO

•• THE FINISH LINE ••

March 20, 2016

While I wrote this entry leading up to Easter, no matter what time of year you're reading it, I hope you are inspired to remember how God made a way for the whole world to be saved.

Will you pause to consider Jesus's unwavering commitment to complete the course set before Him and to finish His mission to redeem all mankind back to God?

On Palm Sunday He experienced a King-worthy entrance into Jerusalem, yet approached it in *humility*. Hours before His death, He shared a quiet last supper with His closest friends, yet comforted *them*. In the garden He agonized in prayer over His Father's will, yet chose to *obey* Him. He endured the betrayal of a friend, yet *healed* a member of his arresting mob. He experienced the utter humiliation, pain, and suffering of a cruel and inhumane death, yet on the cross He asked His Father to *forgive us!*

Jesus Christ, hanging on a Roman cross, finished His mission and with His last breath declared: "It is finished" (John 19:30). In an instant, the "whole of time and eternity" pivoted.*

He saved us! Not only to give us eternal life, but abundant life here and now. He saved us! Not only to pivot *away* from sin, but to empower us *toward* the "finish line." He saved us! That's worth praising Him for this week!

If you're a believer, you're on your course and the finish line is in view. But remember, how you live today will determine how you spend eternity. Doesn't that encourage you to totally abandon yourself to the cause of Christ? To fling yourself in reckless confidence on God? To deny your "self" and live completely for Him? After all He's done for us, isn't He worth it?

I think so! His redeeming love has so captured me, that when my life is over I want to enter Heaven like I just rounded third base in a dead sprint, barreling into home plate yelling, "I'm coming home!" My clothes are torn, my face is bloodied, my body is bruised and scarred, and I'm *just all tore up!* Then I can say, like the apostle Paul, "I have fought the good fight. I have finished the race. I have kept the faith" (2 Tim. 4:7).

As we enter holy week, it would be easy to "practice religion," but will you also honor God by spending personal time with Him, reflecting on all He's done for you and praising Him for saving you? My prayer is that you'll meet Him in a fresh way, so that when your race is over, Heaven will be celebrating at the finish line.

And if you get there first…come cheer me on, cause *I'm coming home!*

---

*Chambers, Oswald, *My Utmost For His Highest*, Uhrichsville, Ohio (1963) p. 128

"He is not here; He has risen!"

Luke 24:6

MT. SHUKSAN, WASH.

•• THE RISING SON ••

> March 27, 2016 <

Early one morning, my friend and I went to the North Cascades of Washington State to watch the sun rise over Mount Shuksan.

After a quick coffee run, we continued our adventurous drive, anticipating the beauty of one of the most photographed vistas in America.

We arrived in plenty of time and were the only members in the audience this early fall morning. Patiently waiting, we strolled around Picture Lake, taking photos as the skies lightened to reveal God's majestic mountain. Slowly, the reflection in the lake began to mirror the strength, peace, and beauty of this awesome sight. We stood still and positioned ourselves for the grand finale, then saw what we came for: the rising sun.

When looking back at photos of that morning, it made me think of another rising sun.

More than two thousand years ago, led by faith, some of Jesus's friends also rose at sunrise. Alone at dawn, a few women approached the tomb where Jesus was buried to see if the Son of God would rise, just as He had said. What they found was miraculous!

"Why do you look for the living among the dead? He is not here; He has risen!" (Luke 24:5–6).

He has risen! God's son rose from the dead just as He had said! And because He rose on Easter morning, His miraculous victory not only gives us the promise of eternity in Heaven but power to live Christ-like here on earth.

The Holy Spirit showed me that just as Picture Lake is positioned to reflect Mount Shuksan's features, we too are positioned to reflect Jesus's nature in us. Like a mighty mountain, He is bold and beautiful, massive and glorious, somewhat imposing and spectacular all in one! But He is also humble and kind, gentle and patient, forgiving, and full of grace and mercy. Because of who He is, shouldn't we be the same?

When arriving that morning, we were rather surprised at how small Picture Lake was. We thought it would take a much larger body of water to reflect such a majestic mountain! Yet couldn't the same be said of the sojourners who are walking by faith? When we love Jesus and live humbly in His reflection, sometimes it only takes one small lake—or one abandoned life—to create a *big* impact.

Will you live humbly this week and allow Christ's nature to be reflected in you? You never know. Your one abandoned life may have a big impact on someone else's eternity.

As for God, His way is perfect.
Psalm 18:30

GOLD BEACH, ORE.

•• THE GOD PARTICLE ••

> April 3, 2016 <

While on a plane to Chicago, I noticed a magazine advertisement for the CERN collider, the world's largest and most powerful particle collider ever built, with the tag line "Decades of patient investment, for a moment of divine clarity."

I paused to consider what this meant, not just for the scientists in search of the "God particle," but for my own journey. There are areas in my faith in which I've endured decades of (impatient) waiting in pursuit of a moment of divine clarity. And like the collider, I've been running in circles chasing after God asking, *"How? Why? When?"*

True to His nature, He didn't answer my questions but led me to *know* Him. And when I began knowing Him, everything changed.

Getting to know God has been a process, but in the process, I found my moment of divine clarity, my secret to patience—*it's what you do while you wait.* It was like discovering my God particle: Patience!

When I filled my "wait time" with seeking God, worshiping Him, and serving and loving others, I began developing patience.

At first, this wasn't easy. I was relearning how to think, taking every thought captive to discipline my mind, and even denying my flesh. But ultimately it's been for the best. How?

The more I waited on Him, the more I trusted Him. And the more I trusted Him, the more I began seeking His face, and not His hand. I wanted to *know* Him and didn't want *something* from Him. Waiting ultimately taught me that to know Him is to trust Him completely with my life.

God is trustworthy. He is full of love and grace. He gives us peace in our storms and turns our sorrow into laughter. He bottles every tear and sees every injustice. His promises are true, and He is faithful to forgive. His power is made perfect in our weakness, and He makes us more than conquerors through Jesus Christ! When we learn to wait patiently, our character is permeated by His character and He keeps us in perfect peace. The Bible says, "As for God, His way is perfect" (Ps. 18:30). When we trust Him, we know He is always working for our good, despite what we see.

What are you doing while you wait? Filling your void with friends and family, adventure and entertainment? Distracting yourself with excessive time on social media? "Doing" things for God instead of "seeking" Him? In your pursuit of the "God particle," will you learn to know Him while you wait?

This may be the week that you "collide" with Him!

...THANKS BE TO GOD!
HE GIVES US THE VICTORY THROUGH
OUR LORD JESUS CHRIST.
1 CORINTHIANS 15:57

DIABLO LAKE, NORTH CASCADES, WASH.

•• THE LAST SHOT ••

April 10, 2016

My mouth dropped open and my arms shot in the air as the clock ticked 0.0 seconds. I had just witnessed Villanova's men's basketball team's last shot that gave them one of the most memorable wins in NCAA men's basketball history!

As I celebrated with fans in Houston's NRG Stadium, I noticed that our look of shock and awe said it all. Did that really happen? Just game-seconds earlier, the pendulum had shifted in the University of North Carolina's favor, when they tied the game with 4.7 seconds remaining. But the game wasn't over. There was time for one more play and that play made sports history!

I left the stadium thinking how the "SuperNova" win paralleled life. There are seasons in our lives when it looks like the game is over. There's no hope that our circumstances will change, no solution to our problem, no comfort for our pain, no vision for our future.

This thinking is right out of Satan's playbook. He wants us to believe that what we see is what we get, that our dreams are dead, that our story is already written. He wants us to give up hope.

But God.

The Bible reminds us that because of Jesus's victory on the cross, we are empowered to live victoriously. "O Death, where is your sting? O Hades, where is your victory? The sting of death is sin…but thanks be to God! He gives us the victory through our Lord Jesus Christ" (1 Cor. 15:55–57).

We win! And we receive our "championship" crown when we enter Heaven.

Until that day, there will be times we give up points, don't follow the game plan, or get absorbed with our "star" power. We will allow temptation to lead us into sin, invite distractions to keep us from knowing God, or believe Satan's lie that God is not good.

When we yield ourselves to God and stay committed to His plan, no matter how long we "sit on the bench," today could be the day He calls our number to take the last shot that changes everything.

So remember, your *game* isn't over until He says it's over.

"OVERCOMING TIME"

TIME DOES ITS BEST,
TO PUSH AND PULL,
DERAIL AND DESTRUCT,
CONSUME AND FOOL.

BUT TIME DOESN'T FOOL ME.
NOT ANYMORE.
GOD CONTROLS TIME,
AND HE'S THE BOSS OF ME.
SO I'M NOT CONTROLLED BY TIME;
I CAN LET LIFE BE.

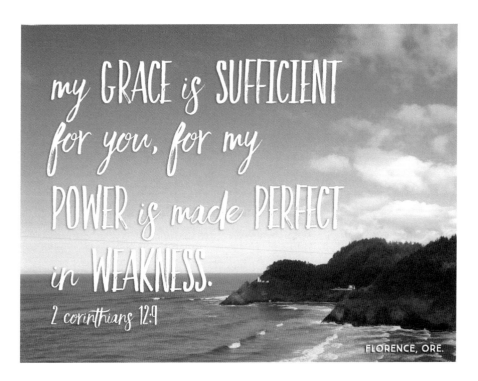

my GRACE is SUFFICIENT for you, for my POWER is made PERFECT in WEAKNESS.

2 corinthians 12:9

FLORENCE, ORE.

•• HELP ME, JESUS! ••

> April 17, 2016

I thought twice before asking a friend to pray for me this particular week.

Prior to reaching out, Satan hit me with a flood of opposition: Why are you asking for prayer? What will your friend think? Aren't you supposed to have it all together, especially after this incredible journey of faith?

I shot back, "I'm asking because my heart hurts and I'm struggling."

Help me.

Oftentimes, to survive our life circumstances we become independent and self-sufficient. Along the way we create the image of "having it all together" when the truth is we don't have to carry that weight. God built us to be vulnerable—to need each other—to share our disappointments, our struggles, our pains and hurts. Most importantly, He created us to need His Son, Jesus.

Help me, Jesus.

If you're like me, vulnerability doesn't come easily. I'm strong—sometimes too strong—but on this particular day I decided I needed help. After all, how could I have it all together? I was coming off an intense two-week business trip across the country; I was without clear direction in my life, and in six weeks I was taking another giant leap of faith and becoming "homeless" again. The truth is I was scared.

God promises us in 2 Corinthians 12:9–10, "My grace is sufficient for you, for my power is made perfect in weakness…For when I am weak, then I am strong."

I considered how this applied to my circumstance, and the Holy Spirit gently revealed my weakness: How can I experience Jesus's sufficient grace and know Him as the strong leader in my life when I remain self-sufficient? How can I trust Him to help me when I won't give Him the opportunity? How can I experience the support of others when I don't let them? When will I stop being the girl who has all the answers and solves all her own problems?

Help me, Jesus!

It's a pithy yet powerful prayer.

Do you need Jesus in your life? Are you practicing vulnerability with Him? If we keep thinking we have it all together, then why would we need Jesus to save us, strengthen us, or display His power in our lives?

I encourage you to be vulnerable this week with Jesus and others. You may need to step out of your comfort zone, but take courage! I'll be praying you'll experience the love and support of Jesus Christ and those around you!

GOD IS THE
STRENGTH OF
MY HEART...

PSALM 73:26

MT. PILCHUCK, WASH.

•• STRENGTH OF MY HEART ••

April 24, 2016

Before finishing a call with me, my friend asked, "What's one thing I can pray for you?"

After talking through my answer, I requested prayer for *strength* to go wherever God may lead.

All week I pondered my reply. How did I come to ask for strength? I didn't ask for direction where to live, for new opportunities, or some great revelation about my future. I asked for God's strength for the journey ahead.

In a way it was a blessing. The Holy Spirit revealed the work He had done in my life. I wasn't asking Him to be my genie-in-a-bottle provider, but I was learning to trust Him with my desires, knowing His way is perfect. I was growing stronger in my faith as He was preparing, leading, and empowering me to serve Him and others.

His revelation reminded me of one of my favorite verses: "My heart and my flesh may fail, but God is the strength of my heart and my portion forever" (Psalm 73:26).

No doubt, I had plenty of life experiences where my heart and flesh had failed! By God's grace, I found *His* strength in my heart when I began seeking and spending extended time with Him. And now only by walking in *His* strength could I serve Him faithfully, remain loyal to His plans, and focus my eyes on the finish line: eternity.

God's *strength of my heart* is all I need to live in the center of His perfect and amazing will for my life!

If you asked for prayer, what would it be? Would you ask for an easier, more fulfilling life? A trouble-free job? A bigger home? Better coworkers? Or would you see your one prayer as a way for God to make your life how *He* wants it, not how *you* want it? Would you allow the Holy Spirit to lead you to the place where you aren't praying for your desires to be filled; rather that you desire to be one with Him so He can fulfill His purpose and plans for you?

Don't be surprised if you feel opposed. Satan is the ultimate heartbreaker. He'll whisper lies of discouragement, distract you from serving Jesus and others, and turn your eyes toward "self." This form of casual Christianity will keep you treating God as a part of your life, not your whole life. So don't let the enemy derail your faith!

My heart is stirred to encourage you in your walk. Rise up, my friends! Raise the bar in your spiritual life. Ask God for His abundant strength to be light in dark places, to bring hope to the hopeless and to know peace in uncertainty. This is no time to back down. Take an inventory of your life and remove everything that is not of Christ: materialism, selfish living, fear of the future, and the cares of this world.

When you do, you'll discover that God is the strength of your heart too. Will you trust Him to lead you into His plans and purposes this week? Open your heart to find out!

Praise be to God...
Psalm 66:20

BIG SUR, CALIF.

• • PAUSING TO PRAISE • •

> May 1, 2016 <

One Sunday afternoon the Holy Spirit presented me with an opportunity to abandon myself to His will. By His strength, I was able to say yes and was blessed with a moment of divine clarity to guide my next step. I was also able to spend quality time with friends, enjoy strong runs in God's nature, and have a very productive workweek.

While any number of those moments could have inspired a blog, I decided to press pause and give praise to God for who He is and for His powerful Word. I would be lost and void of all hope if not for His promises in the Bible that strengthen my faith. His Words have transformed me and empowered me to live a supernatural life! And for that, I give Him praise:

He rescued me from religion and unleashed me into a life of wild and undomesticated faith.

> **Galatians 5:1:** "It is for freedom that Christ has set us free. Stand firm, then, and do not let yourselves be burdened again by a yoke of slavery."

He romanced me across His beautiful country through His mysterious ways!

> **Proverbs 3:5–6:** "Trust in the Lord with all your heart, and lean not on your own understanding. In all your ways acknowledge Him and He will make your paths straight."

He coordinated hundreds of divine appointments to speak truth and hope and life to those He loves.

> **Luke 10:2–3:** "[Jesus] told them, 'The harvest is plentiful, but the workers are few. Ask the Lord of the harvest, therefore, to send out workers into His harvest field. Go! I am sending you out like lambs among wolves.'"

He filled me with His supernatural peace.

> **Philippians 4:6–7:** "Do not be anxious about anything, but in everything, by prayer and petition, with thanksgiving, present your requests to God. And the peace of God, which transcends all understanding, will guard your hearts and your minds in Christ Jesus."

He strengthened me in times of suffering and doubt.

> **Philippians 4:11, 13:** "For I have learned to be content whatever the circumstances…I can do everything through Him who gives me strength.

He was always faithful and never let me go.

> **Matthew 28:20:** "And surely I am with you always, to the very end of the age."

Jeremiah 29:12–14: "'Then you will call upon me and come and pray to me, and I will listen to you. You will seek me and find me when you seek me with all your heart. I will be found by you,' declares the LORD."

I've learned to know Him as my Father and friend; provider and protector; Savior and King. He's cared for and comforted me through seasons of sadness, but praise God! He has more plans and purposes for me just over the horizon!

I love Him! With all my wild heart, my freed mind, and my strengthened body. He is everything to me, and this day I just want to give Him praise. Will you pause to praise Him too?

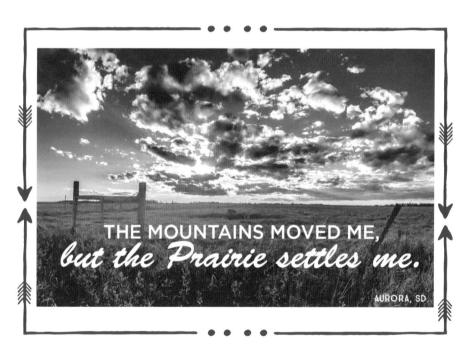

THE MOUNTAINS MOVED ME, *but the Prairie settles me.*

AURORA, SD

Her children arise and call her blessed.

Proverbs 31:28

SKAGIT VALLEY, WASH.

•• HONORING HERITAGE ••

> May 8, 2016 <

Count yourself blessed if you've met my mom. If you *know* her, well then, you know one of God's favorites!

Raised on a small farm in Michigan, she was her father's daughter and enjoyed a hard day's work in the field while also helping in the kitchen and becoming an accomplished seamstress. She set out for Central Bible College filled with divine courage, earning her degree in Bible before returning to Michigan, where she offered her talents as the church pianist, choir director, musical writer, and Sunday school teacher.

She was married with two daughters by age thirty, and her mothering skills blossomed. She simultaneously developed her creative skills, building her own Garden of Eden—beautiful enough to be included on a tour of homes—and establishing herself as the go-to person for interior decorating in her extensive circle of friends.

While she's faithfully multiplied her talents, my mom is admired above all for the *heritage* she offers, a heritage rooted in a relationship with Jesus Christ. Her devotion to her Savior and growing passion for "His Kingdom come" through her life sets the example for us all.

What's her secret to building this heritage? My mom makes a daily choice to live as a humble servant. She's a worshiper at heart, and a behind-the-scenes prayer warrior. My mom reads the word of God *daily*—always has since I can remember! She's devoted to service in the church and to others, denies herself, and puts others first. She ignores the ways of the world and focuses on her Creator, accomplishing His will, not hers.

Love defines my mom! The love of God flows through her, a deep, secure, long-suffering love that is felt by all, but mostly children. She jokes that God is putting her in charge of the nursery in Heaven, but we all know she'll spend just as much time in His garden! She cares for her family and friends, has a contagious laugh, and always lends her hands freely to those in need.

It's because of her incredible sacrifice and inspiring walk of faith that I practiced Proverbs 31:28 this Mother's Day: "Her children arise and call her blessed."

I dedicate this blog to you, Momma. You've stuck with me through all the job changes, the heartbreaks, and the mysterious adventures. You always answered the phone, sent thoughtful notes of encouragement, and have been my biggest supporter. Your gentle words of wisdom, soft rebukes, and loud cheers have helped me develop into who I am today.

While my last few years are so far off the radar—neither one of us knows what to think—I'm most thankful that you trusted me when I was trusting God. What an incredible heritage you've given me. I can only hope to establish the same heritage and impact the world for God's kingdom too!

So this morning, your (favorite) daughter is shouting all the way from Idaho to Michigan: Happy Mother's Day! I love you with all my heart.

To all moms—both physical and spiritual—we arise today and call you blessed!

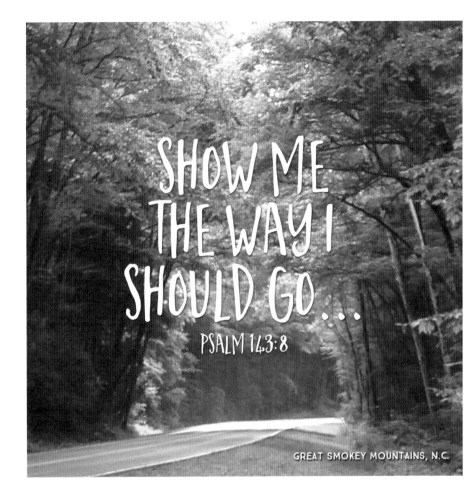

SHOW ME THE WAY I SHOULD GO...

PSALM 143:8

GREAT SMOKEY MOUNTAINS, N.C.

• •FILLING IN THE BLANKS• • ---

May 15, 2016

I stared at the blinking cursor that was impatiently waiting for my input. I was completing a multicity-travel request form and came to my last departure line: June 27, 2016, New York to...blink, blink, blink.

New York to...where?

After obeying the Holy Spirit's leading to give away my possessions again, beginning that next weekend, I would be without a home. While I trusted He was perfectly navigating my waters—freeing me to live in Chicago for a month to work the COPA America Centenario soccer tournament, then finishing my contract in New Jersey working the finals—the reality was I had nowhere to go...yet everywhere to go! As I stared at the blinking cursor, I wondered: where will He lead me next?

I turned away to think and caught a glimpse of His glowing sunset. I bolted out of my apartment and chased the setting sun over the fields. As I ran, the Holy Spirit spoke: "Your heart and mind and body have been renewed to be God's vessel. All the work He's done has been to equip you for the next season in your life, fulfilling His purposes, not yours."

Armed with this reminder, I approached an inviting rock, sat down, and prayed: "God, I'll keep working for you. I'll go wherever you need me. You've faithfully led me and proved yourself trustworthy. I understand my life isn't about me, so all I ask is that you *lead me where you need me*. As long as I have you, I'm good. Just keep leading me and showing me the way."

And He did.

On the day I posted this blog, I couldn't share where. Not because I didn't want to, but because I didn't know: *I was letting Him fill in the blank.*

What I did know is that I had His promises to stand on:

> **ISAIAH 49:23**: "Then you will know that I am the LORD; those who hope in me will not be disappointed."

> **ISAIAH 50:10**: "Let him who walks in the dark, who has no light, trust in the name of the LORD and rely on his God."

> **PSALM 143:8, 10**: "Show me the way I should go, for to you I lift up my soul...Teach me to do your will, for you are my God; may your good Spirit lead me on level ground."

> **MICAH 7:7-8**: "But as for me, I watch in hope for the LORD, I wait for God my Savior; my God will hear me...Though I sit in darkness, the LORD will be my light.

Even though I sat in darkness, I chose to put my hope in Him; to rely on Him; to trust that He heard me and would light my way!

Do you trust your life in God's hands? Or are you impatient with His timing, anxiously filling in the blanks?

My prayer is that you'll stop rushing through life and make a choice to slow down and begin to know God intimately. Trust Him by giving Him room to work in your life. It's as simple as opening your Bible every day and inviting Him in.

While I could have filled in my travel request form with any destination in the country, I practiced patience and left it blank, giving God room so He could lead me in His timing. Will you let God fill in your blanks too?

"LET IT BE"

"I ONCE WAS LOST,
BUT NOW I'M FOUND"
ARE MORE THAN WORDS
FOUND IN A SONG.

THEY'RE LIFE TO THOSE
WHO LIVE THOSE WORDS.
THEY'RE LIFE TO THOSE
WHO KNOW THEIR WORTH.

TRUST IN JESUS.
LET IT BE.
LOVE HIM MORE
THAN ANYTHING.

THE WORLD IS FULL
OF LIES AND TRUTH.
IT'S UP TO YOU
WHICH ONE YOU'LL
CHOOSE.

IF YOU GIVE HIM ROOM
TO LEAD YOUR WAY,
HE'LL FILL YOUR BLANKS
TURN YOUR DARK TO DAY.

TRUST IN JESUS.
LET IT BE.
LOVE HIM MORE
THAN ANYTHING.

WHEN YOUR END IS HERE,
WHEN YOUR DAYS ARE DONE,
WHEN YOUR TIME HAS COME,
HEAR HIM SAY,
"WELL DONE."

"He will quiet you with His love."

Zephaniah 3:17

SHASTA BUTTE, IDAHO

•• QUIET LOVE ••

> May 22, 2016 ⟨

My soul was quiet this week.

Life went on as usual. I made my normal rounds hiking, running, and exploring to counterbalance another intense workweek, but my personal time with God was unusually quiet.

I couldn't put my finger on it until taking a walk on Friday evening and asking what He wanted me to share in this week's blog. I let Him know, "I don't have anything to say!" and for the first time considered not writing one at all as I listened for His leading.

While reflecting on my time with Him, I concluded we were just quiet this week. And then I realized that's what He wanted me to share: the value of being quiet with God.

God already knows me intimately, so when I choose to be quiet, I enjoy the security of His love. This was one of those weeks when I just enjoyed being with Him, knowing He loves me perfectly.

While I've learned many lessons on this journey, learning to be quiet with God produced the greatest changes in my life. Because I know I'm loved, I'm walking in supernatural peace, enjoying His mysterious ways, overcoming sorrows, conquering fears, and renewing my hope in Him. I'm finding strength to live by faith, inspiration to give generously, and assurance to love with abandon!

Most importantly, when I'm quiet I hear His voice. This particular week I struggled with doubt, so I quietly asked for clarification. Immediately, He brought to mind one of His promises. Laughing out loud, I gave thanks that He hears *and* answers the prayers of my heart!

Do you know how to be quiet with God? It starts with a *decision* to pull away from your daily distractions. It takes *discipline* to intentionally seek Him and a strong *determination* to stay in your quiet place.

I encourage you to open your Bible and spend quiet time with God this week. Zephaniah 3:17 promises us, "He will quiet you with His love." Let His Word be planted in your soul so you can reap His love and goodness, perfect guidance, and abundant peace this week!

And that's all I have to say.

THE LORD BLESS YOU AND KEEP YOU;
THE LORD MAKE HIS FACE SHINE UPON YOU
AND BE GRACIOUS TO YOU;
THE LORD TURN HIS FACE TOWARD YOU
AND GIVE YOU PEACE.

NUMBERS 6:24-26

MY FAVORITE FIELD IN IDAHO

•• LOOKING AHEAD ••

May 29, 2016

And so after six months and twenty-six *Where He Leads* blog entries, the Holy Spirit asked me to press pause.

I spent the next month traveling between Chicago and New Jersey working on the COPA America Centenario soccer tournament. With a week to spare, the Holy Spirit revealed that on our upcoming anniversary June 29, 2016, our three-year mission trip would come to an end.

"Where do you want to celebrate?" He asked.

"I'd like to finish how I started," I said, and so I filled in the blank: "Gainesville, Florida."

I spent the next three weeks visiting friends in Florida, continuing to live the mystery of each day, and after quieting myself at my friend's Ponte Vedra Beach home, I received divine inspiration: It's time to move on. Let's camp our way back to Idaho!

Equipping myself with a rental car and an REI tent-package deal, I began what would be a month-long, fourteen-state, forty-seven-hundred-mile summer adventure! Along the way I reconnected with Jesus friends in Brookings, South Dakota, and felt the nudge to set down roots in their beautiful community which is where I currently reside.

REFLECTION

Never could I ever have imagined when I repented and recommitted my life to Jesus that you would be holding this book; a testimony of His power working through my abandoned life. I am a humbled servant, a survivor of His wilderness, a soul on fire to testify to the goodness of Jesus Christ's redeeming love and grace. In response all I can say is *to God be the glory, great things He has done!*

AURORA, S.D.

EPHESIANS 3:20-21: "Now to Him who is able to do immeasurably more than all we ask or imagine, according to His power that is at work within us, to Him be glory in the church and in Christ Jesus throughout all generations, for ever and ever!"

PLAN OF SALVATION

⸻ ••PLAN OF SALVATION•• ⸻

Before continuing on, it's important to take an inventory of your own spiritual life.

Giving your heart to Jesus is the most important decision you will ever make. When you understand your need for His salvation and respond by confessing your sins and inviting Him to be your Lord and Savior, your life as a believer begins!

Understanding your need for Christ's redemption is the first step. What is redemption? I think Oswald Chambers explains it best:

> Redemption means that Jesus Christ can put into any man the hereditary disposition that was in Himself...The moral transaction on my part is agreement with God's verdict on sin in the Cross of Jesus Christ.
>
> God cannot put into me, a responsible moral being, the disposition that was in Jesus Christ unless I am conscious I need it.*

Will you pause for a moment and reflect whether you understand your need for Christ's redemption?

If you are like me, even though I gave my heart to Christ at the age of seven, I came to the realization that my lifestyle of casual faith was actually leading me away from Christ. It was a dangerous road! I had been a believer for over twenty-five years and still didn't grasp my need until I began to call out sin as "sin" in my life. I was desperate for Christ to put His disposition in me.

I am so grateful the Holy Spirit led me to understand my need. In response, I repented and recommitted my life to Him. And on that day my life began to change.

If I had one prayer, it's that you would understand your need for Jesus Christ. My stories and experiences, encouragement and inspiration in this book would all be for nothing if your heart and spirit haven't been stirred to *know* your need for Christ's redemption.

If you haven't given your life to Christ or if you have but your casual life of faith is leading you away from Him, I encourage you to commit to the life Jesus is offering you today. Let today be the day you encounter Christ's love, and allow His love to change you. Will you pray this prayer and invite Him to be Lord of your life?

Dear Lord Jesus, I know that I am a sinner, and I ask for Your forgiveness. I believe You died for my sins and rose from the dead. I turn from my sins and invite You to come into my heart and life. I want to trust and follow You as my Lord and Savior. In Your Name I pray. Amen.

If you've prayed this prayer, will you reach out to another believer and share your experience with him or her? It's important to connect and fellowship with your new family as you begin your walk with Jesus Christ!

Welcome to the family of God!

*Chambers, Oswald, *My Utmost For His Highest*, Uhrichsville, Ohio (1963) p. 280

··SEEK & SPEND··

··SEEK & SPEND··

A guide to *seeking* God with all your heart by *spending* extended time with Him.

I hope you found the blogs inspiring, thought provoking, and challenging as you've considered your own walk of faith. Now it's your turn! What follows are a few ideas to inspire you to take your first step toward knowing God more deeply and becoming a true follower of Christ!

Every journey begins with a first step.

I took my first step in 2008 when I repented and recommitted my life. I made a choice to turn *from* a lifestyle of casual faith and turn *toward* an intimate relationship with Jesus Christ. I began by seeking God with all my heart and learned how to spend extended time with Him. These first steps to living an abundant life of faith forever changed the course of my life!

Those first steps required lifestyle changes. The Holy Spirit began challenging my habits, thought patterns, relationships, priorities, finances, entertainment choices, diet and exercise patterns, among other areas. I say "challenge" because God gives us a free will, and it's our choice to respond to His voice and make the changes necessary that lead us to know Him more intimately.

Spoiler alert: These choices are really personal sacrifices.

Jesus teaches, "Whoever wants to be my disciple must deny themselves and take up their cross daily and follow me" (Luke 9:23).

I always struggled to understand this verse until the Holy Spirit challenged me with its truth. First, was I willing to completely surrender my life to become a disciple/follower of Christ? Second, was I willing to deny my desires, my dreams and my right to myself? And third, was I willing to carry my cross (a deep sorrow in my heart) so He could fulfill His purposes through me? In other words, was I willing to completely abandon my life?

Tough questions! But the sooner I began responding to His challenges by denying myself—ridding myself of old habits, poor choices, and sin—I was making room to know Him better. And the more I knew Him, the greater revelation I had of His peace, joy, love, rest, wisdom, and guidance. Ultimately, knowing His character, His heart, and His nature led me to trust Him with my life. In the end, it's a small sacrifice with a big reward!

—————— • • • • ——————

As you begin your journey to really know God, I encourage you to believe that He will reveal Himself to you through the Holy Spirit. *This is very important.* Believing that you hear from Him will bring you courage to walk confidently in faith—without knowing or seeing—as He leads you into His plans and purposes that will bring Him glory.

I believe that since this book is in your hands, He is stirring something in your spirit. You've heard His call. He's inviting you to participate in His work, and you want to respond. But you don't know how.

Grab your Bible and read on friends! Let's adventure together as you take a first step to becoming a follower of Christ!

Prepare and equip yourself to spend time with Him.

Seeking God is intentional. You're deciding to pursue Him, so it's important to honor Him by showing up prepared and equipped.

Preparing simply means being intentional in setting aside time to meet with Him. He is worthy of every minute of our day, every thought pattern, every choice we make, and every word we speak. So adjusting your schedule, letting friends and family know you're not available, and committing to not look at social media or respond to e-mails and texts is a small sacrifice compared to the opportunity to commune with the King of Kings! When we honor Him in this way, we're preparing our hearts to worship Him for who He is, and intentionally tilling the ground of our souls to receive a word from Him. Beware of distractions and prepare your mind to deny everything that will deter you.

If preparing is setting aside time to enter into communion with God, then equipping yourself is giving you the tools you need to stay in that communion.

When you show up to meet Him with your Bible, you're on the right path. Reading and studying God's Word daily is the greatest tool you have to know Him. He speaks through His Word, providing encouragement, hope, guidance, wisdom, peace, and much more. Whether you're reading how He cared for a widow and her son by filling her jar with oil; or filled a young shepherd boy with enough courage to kill lions, bears, and then a giant; or how He heard the cry of a childless couple and gave them a son; or empowered simple disciples with enough faith to literally change the course of the world, God's character and love are written all across the Bible's pages to help us know Him.

While I reach for my Bible first every morning, I also bring other "equipment" with me, including my journal, a devotional, and worship music.

JOURNALING: Journaling has been a life-changing tool for me. However, learning *how* to journal wasn't a pretty start. In fact, I had many false starts! Anyone else rip out pages or just throw the whole journal away? I've done both. It was only when I began seeing journaling as a way to worship God—giving thanks and praise for who He is and all He's done—that I began developing a deeper relationship with Him and found my voice. Ultimately, I

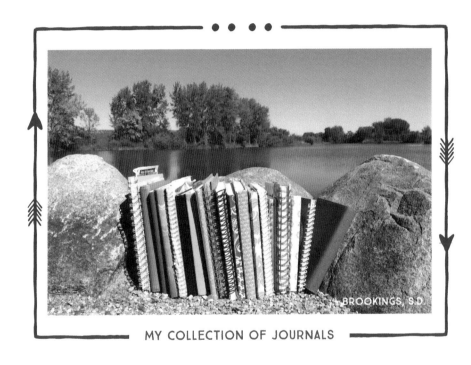

MY COLLECTION OF JOURNALS

learned to become a scribe, writing down what I was hearing from Him. And yes, I still use it to lament, free flow my wandering thoughts, and document my day's interactions and events so I can look back and see all He has done in my life. But most importantly, it's taught me to know Him.

DEVOTIONAL: Equipping myself with a devotional and/or Christian book has also helped me to know God better. It has cast a vision for my life, nurtured my soul, and exposed areas of sin. Oswald Chamber's *My Utmost for His Highest* daily devotional has been by my side for twenty years and, aside from the Bible, has produced the greatest spiritual growth in my life. Oz doesn't mince words! He uses God's truths to rake over my soul, pulling out the dead stuff to allow new spiritual growth. In other words, I highly recommend it (definitely the classic edition. Old school is best!).

WORSHIP MUSIC: And then there's worship music. I love worship music! Since the Bible teaches us to "take captive every thought to make it obedient Christ" (2 Cor. 10:5) and to "be transformed by the renewing of your mind" (Rom. 12:2), listening to worship music has been an incredible tool to help me live by this truth.

If you're like me, you have a thousand thoughts running through your mind each day! Most of the time I'm beating myself up with them, so I've found that playing worship music helps me fight against those thoughts. This is especially important during my devotion times. I'm able to begin by offering thanks and praise which helps me enter into His presence and enjoy the sweet intimacy of His fellowship.

I'll say it again. *Worship music is an incredible tool to keep your mind on Christ!* Not just while meeting with Him, but all day long. I even splurge $3.99 each month for commercial-free Pandora and listen to it in my car, on my portable speaker at home, and through my iPhone on hikes and runs. In other words, I'm a big fan.

● ● ● ●

SOUND LIKE A LOT OF WORK?

You may be thinking: "What difference does it make how I spend my time? Why do I have to prepare? Isn't God with us all the time? Can't I just read a quick ten-minute devotional and be good for the day?"

No.

That's like showing up for a daylong hike in Glacier National Park in flip-flops. If you don't prepare by packing water and snacks and showing up in trail shoes, then you won't get very far. But when you're prepared to spend extended time in the park, then you enjoy the benefit of exploring God's incredible sculpted mountains and pristine glacial lakes, interacting with wildlife, and seeing His beautiful paintings across the skies.

Preparing and equipping yourself to spend a day in the mountains allows you to meet the challenges that strengthen your body and refresh your soul. If you're unprepared and ill-equipped, you'll end up quitting and losing out on the grand experience.

The same could be said of your spiritual life. Do you "show up in flip-flops" each morning, start with good intentions, and then quit? If you're showing up casually to meet with God I challenge you to rethink your approach. He is worthy of all our praise, all our thanks, and all our time! He is the Almighty, your Creator, your Redeemer, the Alpha and Omega, all-powerful, all-knowing and all-loving!

When you intentionally begin to approach Him in humility, surrendering your old life, offering your time, and honoring Him by seeking Him, your real life begins, the day when God will begin His work in you and through you. What a day that will be!

I ENJOYED A 16-MILE HIKE IN GLACIER NATIONAL PARK BY PREPARING AND EQUIPPING MYSELF.

And on that day, you will begin facing a new threat. What do I mean?

I've had the privilege of encountering God's wildlife on my adventures, including numerous bears on my hikes. I say privilege, because it's an exhilarating *I-feel-very-alive* moment that makes your heart beat wildly and your blood pump faster! The fact is, whenever you decide to get out of your car and take a walk in the wild, you will encounter wildlife. After all, you're on their turf, in their environment, walking through their home.

The same could be said about this earth being Satan's turf. He's the prince of this world, and he lurks in the shadows of our life, tracking us and hunting us down. The Bible says he comes to "steal, kill and destroy" (John 10:10), so once you step out of your "car" of comfort and casual faith and step into the wild, he notices.

I believe this is why so many quit in their attempt to seek and spend time with God: they undervalue the power of Satan. He clearly doesn't want us to enter into a deeper relationship with our Creator and will use his weapons. *Distraction*, *doubt*, and *disappointment* are three key areas we all must fight.

The fact is, when you choose to seek God, you're choosing to be tracked by Satan.

Don't be surprised if you decide to wake up early to spend extended time with God and you're met with roadblocks. Maybe you sleep through your alarm or you didn't sleep well the night before and you decide to forgo getting up extra early. Guess who's tracking you.

He tracks to distract.

The good news is when you're prepared and equipped you can overcome the enemy's strategies! Become aware of his ways and you can stay the course.

While there are many ways to spend extended time with God, when I first began, I settled on giving Him the first fruits of my day—my mornings. I found that when I reset my mind at the beginning of a day, allowing Him to fill me up to the point I overflowed with His goodness, then I was ready to start my day. Out of the abundance of what He gave me, I was able to give to others.

After that, I learned how to spend an entire day with God, which eventually led me to venture into unknown paths. As my faith grew over time, I was led by Him on a three-year mission trip across His beautiful land, where I learned to adventure with Him, listening and hearing from Him to take part in His great commission.

This was all a learning process that took place over years, not minutes. I was learning to be led by Jesus's sweet and gentle voice through the Holy Spirit. But just as I grew stronger in climbing steeper paths and running further on trails, I was building up strength and endurance to remain in His presence. This was real living: learning to adventure with Him, worship Him, listen and respond to His leading every moment of my day.

And looking back, it all started with a first step. What will your first step be? I want to encourage you to embrace the beauty of beginning with God: trusting that His way is perfect (Psalm 18:30). Mysterious? Yep, but every day that we learn to embrace His mystery as His way of romancing us, is a day filled with His love and adventure!

With that as a brief background, I'd like to help lead you to know God by seeking Him too! What follows next are a few ideas to kick-start your journey and set you on the path with Jesus Christ.

• • • •

Coffee Lovers

LEARNING TO SEEK GOD IN THE MORNING

In early 2012 I received direction from the Holy Spirit to stop working full-time. I was finishing a contract in Tampa, and on November 1, I would step into the wilderness of an open schedule without a paycheck. This would be a test to see how I spent my time. Would I honor Him by putting Him first, giving Him the first fruits of my day? Yes.

The best decision I made that first day was committing my mornings to seeking God. I walked to Starbucks every morning with my Bible, journal, and devotional and ordered a regular tall coffee (I was on a budget!).

When I sat down, I would open my Bible first to read God's truth. This began a deep hunger to study God's Word that continues to this day. I began realizing just how fascinating the Bible is! It's truly a masterpiece filled with great adventure, endearing love stories, incredible detailed history, creative war strategies, and inspiring poetry.

A key to studying was *slowing down*. I began combing through the gospels, feeding off of Jesus's recorded words and learning to break down the context of what I was reading. I started to wonder about Christ's life, asking the Holy Spirit to reveal new truths. I began seeing how passionately He lived: He fiercely loved His friends; adamantly defended women; joyfully served His Father, whom He deeply loved; sacrificed sleep to rise early and spend time with Him (hint, hint); wisely spoke truths; embraced little children; and was the greatest teacher who ever lived!

Reading His words began to challenge my flesh, exposing areas I needed to surrender, then filled me with His good character. He began challenging my mind and spirit during those mornings. Looking back, He had a plan that would take years, not minutes, to break down my thought patterns, show me I needed to "unlearn" some things, and pull me from a life of busyness and doing things for Him so He could show me the insecurities and doubts that were lurking in my spirit. I've often said it felt like a total renovation of my life—tearing down walls that covered up sin and old thought patterns to expose serious cracks in my foundation!

It's amazing how okay I thought I was until I allowed the Holy Spirit to use the truth of God's Word to tear down these walls. For years, I sought change by attending various churches, seeking out Bible conferences, and reading all kinds of Christian literature. These were all good and beckoned me to know Christ more, but it wasn't until I started feeding off the pure Word of God, surrendering my time and intentionally seeking Him, that I began to see true change happen in my life.

Sound like what you're looking for too?

It can all begin with a cup of coffee with God! It doesn't mean you have to pack it up every morning and go to a coffee shop, but it's important to dedicate a time and place each morning. It may be in your prayer closet, on your deck, in your room, or wherever. The important thing is to start and keep at it. Be patient, be strong enough to deny the distractions, and be consistent in your pursuit. He is faithful and will meet you where you are. Simply invite Him in!

Adventurers

Spending time with God outside has also been key to my spiritual growth. When you decide to intentionally seek Him by stepping away from your familiar surroundings, you're one step closer to knowing Him better! I wish I could go with each of you on your first adventure with God, but I guess the point is that you go with Him, not me!

I found that the key to adventuring with God is believing that you're not alone. Whether you choose to take a slow walk in your local park, go on a long bike ride, hike a mountain, or kayak in new waters, invite Him with you. Talk with Him. Pray for others. Share what's on your heart. Worship Him. Cry it out if you need to! Tell Him what you're feeling and thinking. The point is to build a real relationship with Him, believing that He's with you every step of the way.

When I was living in the wilderness (three years without family and friends), I had some of my most intimate times on these adventures. I had no one else to turn to but Him! I found it incredibly freeing to speak out loud what I was feeling and thinking as if He was in the flesh adventuring with me. Did I have to explain myself to fellow hikers/runners who heard me approaching? You bet! But who cares? I was adventuring with God, and that's all that mattered.

I found these were the best times to thank Him for His creation too. When you slow down, listening to the sounds of nature and intentionally looking for the smallest, most delicate details of His masterpieces, I guarantee you'll be wowed by His creativity!

Whatever you choose to do—no matter if you are fifteen or seventy-five—the point is to get out of your home or car and spend time with Him outside. Even if it's winter, bundle up and get some fresh air. When summer rolls around, pack it up and hit those trails. He is waiting to adventure with you!

WHILE RUNNING THE CENTENNIAL TRAIL IN WASHINGTON, THE SIGHT OF THIS DELICATE MASTERPIECE CAUSED ME TO ABRUPTLY STOP! I WAS FASCINATED THAT EACH NEEDLE GENTLY HELD A DROP OF DEW. MAGNIFICENTLY BEAUTIFUL!

ONE MORE NOTE:

To help me remember and respond to the beauty of God's nature on these adventures, I bring my iPhone to take photos. This is how I captured each of the photos in this book. I also hear clearly from Him and use my phone's notes function to write down what I hear. You may respond to and remember His beauty differently, by drawing, painting, or playing an instrument. Whatever your talent or desire, equip yourself in whichever way you choose to express your appreciation. Enjoy capturing those moments!

Pioneers

LEARNING HOW TO SPEND A DAY WITH GOD

If you're up for this challenge, then you've chosen wisely! There's a hunger inside you to know Him more and by choosing to spend an entire day with God, you are well on your way to a more intimate relationship with Jesus Christ! I love that you're taking deeper steps into the unknown, trusting that you'll figure out this new life as you go!

I clearly remember the first time I committed an entire day to God. It was a beautiful summer Saturday in Tampa. I began my morning with coffee and devotions, then packed a bag and spent the afternoon at Marjorie Park on Davis Islands reading, writing, running and walking around the islands while worshipping and observing God's beauty. I continued through the evening at home and found it to be a great first step to building up an endurance to keep my thoughts on Him and stay in His presence.

When you choose this option, it's important to remember this doesn't have to be epic. My first day with God was spent in my hometown, just five miles from my house. I eventually ventured farther out, but I started at a local park. The purpose of this day is to step into a lifestyle of faith, where you're living out a relationship with God, learning to just be with Him, no matter where you are. Trust me, He's the best company! But just like adventuring with Him, you have to believe that you're not alone. Faith is being sure of what you hope for (that He's with you) and certain of what you do not see (that He's with you) (Heb. 11:1).

Will you set aside a day to spend with Him? Remember what an honor it is to spend time with our Lord Jesus Christ!

Trailblazers

—— LEARNING TO GO WITHOUT KNOWING ——

Welcome to exhilarating faith, my friends! By choosing to step out in faith, you've arrived at a place where you're confident you can hear from the Holy Spirit.

Just like pioneering with God, this doesn't have to be epic. Stepping into the unknown can be as simple as responding in obedience to the Holy Spirit's leading. Maybe He'll ask you to approach your neighbor and ask if he or she needs prayer or lead you to practice generosity when it won't make sense. No matter what He asks, the important lesson is to *go*—do what He's asked without knowing why or how or where!

While my walk of faith eventually led me across the country multiple times, it all began with small steps. When I learned to respond in obedience to the still, small voice of the Holy Spirit, I was being challenged by Him to take to take bigger steps. Ultimately, I learned how to be led day by day, embracing the mystery of His will.

This type of learning was and still is a process. It wasn't until December 2013, when I took my first big step of faith and went on what would become a three-week trip up the East Coast, that I began to see how He works.

I challenged myself to leave Tampa and head north, without any plans, in order to see where He would lead.

What unfolded taught me a great lesson: *we have to participate with God on these journeys.* I was learning to seek His voice, but just as important, He wanted me to respond by engaging in the process. The good news is He often asked me, "What do you want?" In this case, after two weeks on the road, I sat in a rocking chair at the Hershey Hotel and told Him I wanted to go to New York City to see the lights.

Do you know what He said? "Then go!"

With an hour to spare of check out, I packed up my car and headed east, and the most amazing four-day trip unfolded. And then the beauty of His economy happened: when I arrived in New York, I received an unexpected contract to work the NCAA Football Championship in Miami, which ended up covering the entire cost of my trip.

While trailblazing with God on these trips, I was learning what it meant to be sent out on the Great Commission. Hundreds of divine appointments unfolded during the next four years, and I began learning what an honor it was to be used by Him. I was experiencing the thrill of being led to a specific place to meet a specific person at a specific time. In reality, these were and

THIS IS THE ROCKING CHAIR I SAT ON, WAITING TO HEAR FROM THE HOLY SPIRIT

are all mission trips coordinated by the Holy Spirit! And these appointments only happened by stepping out in faith.

When you learn to hear from Him, you begin trusting that at just the right time He will give you words to say or prompt you to do what He asks. Your job is to keep your mind clear of distractions and doubt and live an others-centered life so no matter where you are, you stand ready to be used by God. It's risky, but exhilarating!

Are you ready to *go* without knowing? Get in your quiet place today and ask the Holy Spirit to lead and guide you. And experience the thrill of doing the Father's will!

SIOUX FALLS, S.D.

READY, SET...NOW GO!

While these are just ideas to inspire and help guide you, the Holy Spirit is your most important source of inspiration. Will you let Him lead you to become a follower of Christ?

The Bible says, "Faith comes by hearing and hearing by the word of God" (Rom. 10:17). I encourage you to pick up your Bible today and hear God speak directly to you. Trust Him with your life. Allow Him to make a difference in you so you can make a difference in others' lives too!

MAY YOUR LIGHT SHINE IN DARK PLACES,
THAT YOUR LIGHT,
YOUR ONE LIFE,
MAY AFFECT MANY LIVES FOR ETERNITY.

JOURNAL

I've written how journaling has both strengthened my relationship with Jesus and given me an opportunity to record His story written on my heart. What follows are blank pages for Him to write His story on your heart too. I encourage you to begin by honoring Him and record your thanks and praise for both who He is and all He's done for you. You can follow by documenting your day and/or writing as if you were speaking with Him. Then take time to listen and record what He's speaking to you. I'm excited for you to discover that He speaks!

Enjoy your journey friends. I hope to see you on the trails of Heaven someday!

My life isn't absent of fear; I just don't give it room to breathe.

The purpose of the wilderness
is to become bewildered.

Be the most courageous person you know.

I don't have the luxury of being afraid.

> The better I know God,
> the fewer questions I
> ask. I trust Him.

Don't fear, Jesus is near.

> What you see is temporary.
> What is to come is eternal.

Worship is my water and the
Bible is my bread. I fill my
doubts with both.

> Consider the cost of following Christ. And then consider the cost of NOT following Him.

> My worth to God in public is who I've become in private.

The only time to look back in life is to remember all God has done for you.

I had the fire and desire, but wasn't refined. Let Him take you through His fire and refine you.

Read the Bible for seeds. Allow God time
to cultivate those seeds in your life.

Linger longer in His Presence.

Want to live an exciting life? Get to know the Holy Spirit.

You have to go dark to see the stars. Sometimes you have to walk in that same darkness to see God's handiwork in your life.

BBQ ON HIGHWAY 52
JALAMA BURGER ON THE BEACH
HIGH STREET GRAVEL
SHORTCAKE PLEASE
GRASS FED STEAK AND CATCH OF THE DAY!

ON THE ROAD
TASTING LIFE, TEMPTING TIME
LOOKING BACK, LOOKING AHEAD
TASTING LIFE, LIVING MINE

SURVIVE & THRIVE
SLOW DOWN, ENJOY
LIFE'S NEXT TURN
HAS PLENTY IN STORE

COFFEE SHOPS, HOLE-IN-THE-WALL
OCEANFRONTS, SUMMITS TOO
NO MATTER WHERE
ENJOY THE VIEW

GET UP, GET OUT!
THERE'S PLACES TO GO
SIGHTS TO SEE, WORLDS TO KNOW
LOSE YOUR WAY
GIVE IN, LET GO
TRUST IN GOD
BEGIN TODAY!

GLACIER NATIONAL PARK

Thank you to my parents, Norm and Joan, and my sister Michele, for your gracious love and support while I ventured off on a life of wild and undomesticated faith! Thanks for always believing in me.

To my friend Lynn for sharing your life and teaching me the joy of true friendship. To the Schackows for adopting me into your Gainesville family; your influence has meant more than you know. To Michele D. for capturing my ministry vision and using your talents to bring it to life; and to Carrie for seamlessly grabbing the baton and running with it! To Julie, Amanda and countless friends in Florida for helping me grow into who I am today; to Paul for being my best advocate in Tampa; and to Sharyn for all of the contract opportunities and extending patience while letting God 'fill-in-the-blank'.

I'm grateful to the Hansens in Washington for hosting me in your lovely country home for a year; your family will always hold a special place in my heart (and all your pups too!). To the Cehrs in Idaho for your love and support; to my Coeur d'Alene coffee friends for strengthening my faith; to Amy for your friendship (and author photo!); to the Scotts for including me into your extended family; and to Ryan for helping me stay the course.

To the hundreds of people I've divinely encountered along the way – all I can say is thank you. Whether you knew it or not, you were the reason for this journey.

And finally, to my Creator and the true Lover of my soul, I lift up my eyes and say thank you…*for everything*. My heart aches to see you, but until that day, I venture on to love others with the love you graciously offer me.

Grace and peace to all!